A Cake for You

The Cookbook That Will Enable You to Prepare 100+ Irresistible Recipes at Home That Will Delight Your Palate

Angela Norrel

SPECIAL DISCLAIMER

All the information's included in this book are given for instructive, informational and entertainment purposes, the author can claim to share very good quality recipes but is not headed for the perfect data and uses of the mentioned recipes, in fact the information's are not intent to provide dietary advice without a medical consultancy.

The author does not hold any responsibility for errors, omissions or contrary interpretation of the content in this book.

It is recommended to consult a medical practitioner before to approach any kind of diet, especially if you have a particular health situation, the author isn't headed for the responsibility of these situations and everything is under the responsibility of the reader, the author strongly recommend to preserve the health taking all precautions to ensure ingredients are fully cooked.

All the trademarks and brands used in this book are only mentioned to clarify the sources of the information's and to describe better a topic and all the trademarks and brands mentioned own their copyrights and they are not related in any way to this document and to the author.

This document is written to clarify all the information's of publishing purposes and cover any possible issue.

Table Of Contents

Table Of Contents

Table Of Contents

Applesauce Cake VI

Ingredients

3 cups all-purpose flour
3 teaspoons baking powder
2 teaspoons baking soda
1/2 teaspoon salt
2 teaspoons ground cinnamon
4 eggs
2 cups white sugar
1 1/2 cups vegetable oil
2 cups applesauce
1 teaspoon vanilla extract

Directions

Preheat oven to 350 degrees F (175 degrees C). Grease and flour a 10 inch tube pan. Sift together the flour, baking powder, baking soda, salt and cinnamon. Set aside.

In a large bowl, mix together the flour, baking powder, baking soda, salt and cinnamon. Make a well in the center and pour in the eggs, sugar, oil, applesauce and vanilla. Mix well and pour into prepared pan.

Bake in the preheated oven for 50 to 60 minutes, or until a toothpick inserted into the center of the cake comes out clean. Let cool in pan for 10 minutes, then turn out onto a wire rack and cool completely.

Apple Honey Bundt Cake

Ingredients

1 cup white sugar
1 cup vegetable oil
2 eggs
3/4 cup honey
1 teaspoon vanilla extract
2 1/2 cups all-purpose flour
1 teaspoon baking powder
1 teaspoon baking soda
1 teaspoon salt
1 teaspoon ground cinnamon
1/4 teaspoon ground allspice
3 apples - peeled, cored and shredded
3/4 cup chopped walnuts

Directions

Preheat the oven to 325 degrees F (165 degrees C). Grease and flour a 9 inch Bundt pan.

In a large bowl, stir together the sugar and oil. Beat in the eggs until light, then stir in the honey and vanilla. Combine the flour, baking powder, baking soda, salt, cinnamon and allspice; stir into the batter just until moistened. Fold in the apples and nuts.

Bake for 50 to 65 minutes in the preheated oven, or until a toothpick inserted into the crown comes out clean. Let cool for 10 to 15 minutes before inverting onto a plate and tapping out of the pan.

Ingredients

1 1/2 cups water
1 1/2 cups raisins
3/4 cup dates, pitted and chopped
1 teaspoon baking soda
1/2 cup butter
3/4 cup white sugar
2 eggs
1 teaspoon vanilla extract
1 1/2 cups all-purpose flour
1/4 teaspoon salt

4 tablespoons butter
1/2 cup brown sugar
2 tablespoons heavy cream
1/2 cup chopped walnuts

Directions

Preheat oven to 350 degrees F (175 degrees C). Grease and flour a 9 inch square pan. In a saucepan, combine water and raisins. Bring to a boil and cook for 5 minutes. Remove from heat and stir in chopped dates and baking soda. Set aside.

In a large bowl, cream together 1/2 cup butter and 3/4 cup white sugar until light and fluffy. Beat in the eggs one at a time, then stir in the vanilla. Beat in the flour, salt and date mixture. Pour batter into prepared pan.

Bake in the preheated oven for 45 minutes, or until a toothpick inserted into the center of the cake comes out clean. Remove cake from oven, and set oven to Broil.

Make Topping: In a saucepan, melt 4 tablespoons of butter. Stir in brown sugar, cream and chopped nuts. Spread mixture over warm cake and place under broiler until lightly browned, about 3 minutes. Watch carefully - it burns easily under the broiler. Cool before serving.

My Mom's Apple Sauce Cake

Ingredients

2 1/2 cups all-purpose flour
1/4 teaspoon baking powder
1 1/2 teaspoons baking soda
1 1/2 teaspoons salt
3/4 teaspoon ground cinnamon
1/2 teaspoon ground cloves
1/2 teaspoon ground allspice
1/2 cup shortening
1 cup white sugar
1/2 cup water
1 egg
1/2 cup chopped walnuts
1 cup chopped raisins
1 (16 ounce) jar applesauce

1 (8 ounce) package cream cheese
1 tablespoon milk
1 teaspoon vanilla extract
5 1/2 cups sifted confectioners' sugar
1/3 cup orange juice

Directions

Preheat oven to 350 degrees F (175 degrees C), grease and flour a 9x13 inch pan or 2 - 8 inch round pans.

Sift together flour, baking powder, baking soda, salt, cinnamon, cloves and allspice. set aside.

In a large bowl, cream shortening and sugar until light and fluffy. Mix in water and egg. Add flour mixture alternately with applesauce and mix thoroughly. Fold in nuts and raisins.

Pour into pan and bake at 350 degrees F (175 degrees C) for 45 to 50 minutes or until a toothpick inserted into center of cake comes out clean. Cool and frost with cream cheese frosting.

To make frosting: In a medium bowl, beat cream cheese until smooth. Add milk and vanilla and mix in. Add confectioners sugar and orange or lemon juice. Beat until fluffy, then frost cake.

Cassata Cake

Ingredients

1 1/2 cups cake flour
1/2 teaspoon baking powder
1/4 teaspoon salt
5 eggs
1/2 cup cold water
1 1/4 cups white sugar
1 teaspoon vanilla extract
1/2 teaspoon cream of tartar

2 pounds whole milk ricotta cheese
2 1/4 cups confectioners' sugar
1/2 teaspoon ground cinnamon
1 1/2 teaspoons vanilla extract
2 (1 ounce) squares semi-sweet chocolate
1/2 cup candied lemon peel

1/3 cup white sugar
1/4 cup water
2 tablespoons light rum

6 (1 ounce) squares bittersweet chocolate, chopped
1/3 cup heavy whipping cream
3 tablespoons unsalted butter, cubed

Directions

Preheat the oven to 325 degrees F (165 degrees C). Grease and line with parchment paper 2 nine inch round layer pans.

Sift the flour, baking powder, and salt together.

Separate the eggs and set the egg whites aside. Beat the egg yolks together on medium-high speed until very thick, about 4 minutes. Gradually add the cold water. Add 1- 1/4 cups of the white sugar, slowly, and beat well for about 3 more minutes. Add 1 teaspoon of the vanilla. Sift the flour mixture over the egg yolk mixture and fold in.

Beat the egg whites and cream of tartar together until stiff peaks form. Fold this into the yolk mixture. Divide batter between the pans.

Bake at 325 degrees F (165 degrees C) for 25 minutes. Cool on rack for 10 minutes and then invert and cool completely.

Cut each cake layer in half. Place one of the 4 halves on a cake board or plate and sprinkle with a little of the Rum Syrup. Spread about 1-1/2 cups of the Filling over this layer. Add a second layer of cake and repeat this procedure. Top the cake with the last layer of cake. Chill at least 4 hours. Spread Chocolate Glaze over top of cake.

To Make Ricotta Cheese Filling: Beat the ricotta cheese well and add the confectioner's sugar and cinnamon. Add 1-1/2 teaspoons of the vanilla and grate 2 ounces of the chocolate in using the coarse side of a grater. Stir in the candied lemon peel and mix. Chill until ready to use.

To Make The Rum Syrup: Place 1/3 cup of the sugar and the water in a small saucepan. Bring to a boil over medium heat, stirring to dissolve sugar. Boil 1 minute and then remove from heat and add the rum. Cool to room temperature.

To Make The Chocolate Glaze: Melt 6 ounces of the chocolate and the cream in the microwave, whisk smooth. Add the butter and whisk until dissolved. Cool mixture until spreadable. Spread over the top of the cake.

Chocolate Pudding Cake

Ingredients

1/2 cup biscuit/baking mix
2 tablespoons sugar
2 teaspoons baking cocoa
3 tablespoons milk
1/2 teaspoon vanilla extract
TOPPING:
3 tablespoons brown sugar
1 tablespoon baking cocoa
1/2 cup boiling water
Ice cream or whipped cream
(optional)

Directions

In a small bowl, combine baking mix, sugar and cocoa. Stir in milk and vanilla. Spoon into two greased 8- or 10-oz. custard cups.

For topping, combine the brown sugar and cocoa in a bowl. Stir in boiling water. Pour over batter. Bake at 350 degrees F for 25 minutes or until a toothpick inserted in the cake layer comes out clean. Top with ice cream or whipped cream if desired.

Polish Coffee Cake

Ingredients

2 (.25 ounce) packages active dry yeast
1/4 cup warm water (110 degrees F/45 degrees C)
3 cups milk
1 cup butter
10 eggs, beaten
1 1/2 cups white sugar
1/4 teaspoon ground nutmeg
1/4 teaspoon orange extract
1 1/2 teaspoons vanilla extract
10 cups all-purpose flour
1 teaspoon salt

1/2 cup butter, cubed
2/3 cup white sugar

Directions

In a small bowl, dissolve yeast in warm water. Let stand until creamy, about 10 minutes. Warm the milk in a small saucepan until it bubbles, then remove from heat. Mix in 1 cup butter until melted. Let cool until lukewarm.

In a large bowl, beat together the eggs and 1 1/2 cups sugar. Mix in the nutmeg, orange extract, vanilla extract, and the yeast mixture. Stir in 3 cups flour and the salt. Stir in 1/3 of the milk mixture. Mix in the remaining flour and milk mixture in two alternating additions. Cover bowl, and let rise until doubled, about 45 minutes.

In a small bowl, prepare the topping by cutting together 1/2 cup butter and 2/3 cups sugar until mixture resembles coarse crumbs.

Preheat oven to 350 degrees F (175 degrees C). Lightly grease 3 10-inch Bundt pans.

Divide dough into the prepared pans, and sprinkle with the topping mixture.

Bake in preheated oven for 30 to 40 minutes, until a toothpick inserted into center comes out clean.

Coconut Chocolate Cake

Ingredients

4 eggs
3/4 cup vegetable oil
3/4 cup water
1 teaspoon vanilla extract
1 (18.25 ounce) package chocolate cake mix
1 (3.9 ounce) package instant chocolate pudding mix
FILLING:
2 cups flaked coconut
1/3 cup sweetened condensed milk
1/4 teaspoon almond extract
1 (16 ounce) container chocolate frosting

Directions

In a mixing bowl, beat the eggs, oil, water and vanilla. Add the cake and pudding mixes; beat for 5 minutes. Pour 3 cups into a greased and floured 10-in. fluted tube pan. Combine the coconut, milk and extract; mix well. Drop by spoonfuls onto batter. Cover with remaining batter.

Bake at 350 degrees F for 50-60 minutes or until a toothpick inserted near the center comes out clean. Cool for 10 minutes before removing from pan to a wire rack to cool completely. Frost with chocolate frosting.

Oatmeal Cake II

Ingredients

1 1/4 cups boiling water
1 cup quick cooking oats
1/2 cup butter
3/4 cup packed brown sugar
3/4 cup white sugar
2 eggs
1 teaspoon vanilla extract
1 teaspoon baking soda
1/2 teaspoon salt
1 teaspoon ground cinnamon
1 1/2 cups all-purpose flour
1/2 cup raisins

Directions

Pour the boiling water over the quick oats and let stand for 20 minutes.

Preheat oven to 350 degrees F (175 degrees C). Lightly grease one 13x15 inch baking pan .

Cream the shortening with the sugar until light. Beat in the eggs. Then add the oats and vanilla, mixing well.

Combine the baking soda, salt , cinnamon and flour. Mix until combined. Add the raisins to the flour mixture and coat well.

Add the raisin and flour mixture to the oatmeal mixture and stir to combine. Pour the batter into the prepared pan.

Bake at 350 degrees F (175 degrees C) for 25 minutes or until a tester inserted near the center comes out clean. Dust with confectioners' sugar or serve with whipped topping, if desired.

Ingredients

3 eggs
1 1/4 cups vegetable oil
2 cups white sugar
2 1/2 cups self-rising flour
2 apple - peeled, cored, and chopped
1 cup shredded coconut
1 cup chopped walnuts
1/4 cup butter
1/2 cup packed brown sugar
1/3 cup milk

Directions

Preheat oven to 350 degrees F (175 degrees C). Grease and flour tube or bundt pan.

Blend eggs, oil, and sugar until creamy. Add flour, a little at a time. Blend well. Batter will be stiff. Fold in apples, coconut, and nuts.

Pour into prepared pan. Bake in preheated oven for 60 minutes, or until a toothpick inserted into the center comes out clean. Let cool 30 minutes in pan, then remove.

To Make Topping: Melt butter or margarine, sugar, and milk in saucepan over high heat. Bring to boil for 3 minutes. Pour over cooled cake.

Something Different Pound Cake

Ingredients

1 cup butter
1/2 cup shortening
3 cups white sugar
5 eggs
3 cups all-purpose flour
1/2 teaspoon salt
1/2 teaspoon baking powder
1/2 cup milk
1/2 cup evaporated milk
1 teaspoon rum flavored extract
1 teaspoon coconut extract

1 cup white sugar
1 teaspoon rum flavored extract
1 teaspoon coconut extract
1 teaspoon almond extract
1/2 cup water

Directions

Preheat oven to 325 degrees F (165 degrees C). Grease a 10 inch tube pan and line with parchment paper. Grease the parchment paper. Sift flour, salt and baking powder together and set aside.

In a large bowl, cream butter, shortening and 3 cups sugar until light and fluffy. Add eggs one at a time, beating well after each. Add 1 teaspoon rum extract and 1 teaspoon coconut extract. Add flour mixture alternately with milk and evaporated milk. Mix until smooth.

Pour batter into 10 inch tube pan. Bake at 325 degrees F (165 degrees C) for 1 hour and 15 minutes, or until a toothpick inserted into cake comes out clean. Cool.

Make the glaze: in a saucepan, combine 1 cup sugar, 1/2 cup water, 1 teaspoon rum extract, 1 teaspoon coconut extract and 1 teaspoon almond extract. Bring to a boil, stirring constantly. Use a toothpick to pierce all over the top of the cake. Pour the glaze over the cooled cake and allow it to soak in.

Italian Wedding Cake Martini

Ingredients

2 fluid ounces vanilla vodka
1 fluid ounce cranberry juice
1 fluid ounce pineapple juice 1/2
fluid ounce amaretto (almond
flavored liqueur)
1/2 fluid ounce white creme de
cacao

Directions

Pour the vodka, cranberry juice, pineapple juice, amaretto, and creme de cacao into a cocktail shaker over ice. Cover, and shake until the outside of the shaker has frosted. Strain into a chilled martini glass to serve.

Hot Milk Cake

Ingredients

1/2 cup milk
3/4 cup all-purpose flour
1 teaspoon baking powder
1/4 teaspoon salt
3 eggs, room temperature
1 cup sugar
1 teaspoon vanilla extract
TOPPING:
1/3 cup packed brown sugar
1/2 cup chopped pecans
2 tablespoons butter or margarine, softened
2 tablespoons milk
1 cup shredded coconut

Directions

Scald milk; set aside. Combine flour, baking powder and salt; set aside. in a mixing bowl, beat eggs until thick and lemon-colored. Gradually add sugar, blending well. On low speed, alternately mix in milk, dry ingredients and vanilla. Pour batter into a greased 10-in. cast-iron skillet. Bake at 350 degrees F for 25-30 minutes or until the cake springs back when lightly touched. Remove cake and preheat broiler. Combine all topping ingredients and sprinkle over cake. Broil 5 inches from the heat until topping bubbles and turns golden brown. Serve warm.

German Chocolate Cake III

Ingredients

1/2 cup water
4 (1 ounce) squares German sweet chocolate
1 cup butter, softened
2 cups white sugar
4 egg yolks
1 teaspoon vanilla extract
1 cup buttermilk
2 1/2 cups cake flour
1 teaspoon baking soda
1/2 teaspoon salt
4 egg whites

1 cup white sugar
1 cup evaporated milk
1/2 cup butter
3 egg yolks, beaten
1 1/3 cups flaked coconut
1 cup chopped pecans
1 teaspoon vanilla extract

1/2 teaspoon shortening
1 (1 ounce) square semisweet chocolate

Directions

Preheat oven to 350 degrees F (175 degrees C). Grease and flour 3 - 9 inch round pans. Sift together the flour, baking soda and salt. Set aside. In a small saucepan, heat water and 4 ounces chocolate until melted. Remove from heat and allow to cool.

In a large bowl, cream 1 cup butter and 2 cups sugar until light and fluffy. Beat in 4 egg yolks one at a time. Blend in the melted chocolate mixture and vanilla. Beat in the flour mixture alternately with the buttermilk, mixing just until incorporated.

In a large glass or metal mixing bowl, beat egg whites until stiff peaks form. Fold 1/3 of the whites into the batter, then quickly fold in remaining whites until no streaks remain.

Pour into 3 - 9 inch pans Bake in the preheated oven for 30 minutes, or until a toothpick inserted into the center of the cake comes out clean. Allow to cool for 10 minutes in the pan, then turn out onto wire rack.

To make the Filling: In a saucepan combine 1 cup sugar, evaporated milk, 1/2 cup butter, and 3 egg yolks. Cook over low heat, stirring constantly until thickened. Remove from heat. Stir in coconut, pecans and vanilla. Cool until thick enough to spread.

Spread filling between layers and on top of cake. In a small saucepan, melt shortening and 1 ounce of chocolate. Stir until smooth and drizzle down the sides of the cake.

Yum Yum Cake I

Ingredients

2 cups all-purpose flour
2 1/2 teaspoons baking powder
3/4 teaspoon salt
2/3 cup shortening
1 1/2 cups white sugar
1 tablespoon orange zest
2 teaspoons lemon zest
5 eggs
2/3 cup milk
1/4 cup orange juice
1/4 cup lemon juice
1/4 cup reserved pineapple juice
1 (3.5 ounce) package instant vanilla pudding mix

1 (3.5 ounce) package instant vanilla pudding mix
1 cup milk
1 (8 ounce) package cream cheese
1 (8 ounce) container frozen whipped topping, thawed
1 (15 ounce) can crushed pineapple, drained
10 maraschino cherries, halved

Directions

Preheat oven to 350 degrees F (175 degrees C), grease and lightly flour a 9x13 inch pan.

In a small bowl, mix flour, baking powder and salt. Set aside.

Beat shortening for 30 seconds, add sugar, lemon and orange zest and beat until light and fluffy. Add eggs one at a time, beating well after each. Add pudding mix. Add flour mixture, alternating with milk and juices beating well after each addition.

Pour into pan. Bake at 350 degrees F (175 degrees C) for 30 to 45 or until toothpick inserted into center of cake comes out clean. Cool in pan.

To make the topping: Mix vanilla pudding with milk and set aside. Beat cream cheese until smooth, add cool whip, then pudding and mix on lowest speed until well combined. Spread on top of cooled cake. arrange pineapples and cherries on top.

Country Apple Coffee Cake

Ingredients

2 medium tart apples, peeled and chopped
1 (12 ounce) package refrigerated buttermilk biscuits
1 egg
1/3 cup corn syrup
1/3 cup packed brown sugar
1 tablespoon butter or margarine, softened
1/2 teaspoon ground cinnamon
1/2 cup chopped pecans
GLAZE:
1/3 cup confectioners' sugar
1/4 teaspoon vanilla extract
1 teaspoon milk

Directions

Place 1-1/2 cups apples in a greased 9-in. round baking pan. Separate biscuits into 10 pieces; cut each biscuit into quarters. Place over apples with point side up. Top with remaining apples. In a mixing bowl, combine egg, corn syrup, brown sugar, butter and cinnamon. Stir in pecans. Spoon over apples. Bake at 350 degrees F for 30-35 minutes or until biscuits are browned.

For glaze, combine confectioners' sugar, vanilla and enough milk to achieve desired consistency. Drizzle over warm coffee cake. Serve immediately.

Yum Yum Cake III

Ingredients

1 (8 ounce) can crushed pineapple, drained
1 (18.25 ounce) package yellow cake mix
1 (8 ounce) package cream cheese
1 (3.4 ounce) package instant vanilla pudding mix
1 cup milk
1 (16 ounce) container frozen whipped topping, thawed

Directions

Bake yellow cake mix according to instructions on package in a 15x10 inch jelly roll pan. Allow to cool.

In a medium bowl, combine cream cheese, pudding mix and milk. beat until smooth and spread on cooled cake. Sprinkle drained pineapple on top of pudding.

Spread whipped topping over pineapple. Sprinkle with chopped nuts. Chill in refrigerator.

Peanut Butter and Chocolate Cake I

Ingredients

2 cups cake flour
2 teaspoons baking powder
1/4 teaspoon salt
3/4 cup unsalted butter, softened
1 1/3 cups white sugar
2 eggs
3/4 cup creamy peanut butter
1 tablespoon vanilla extract
1 cup milk

3/4 cup unsalted butter
1 1/4 cups confectioners' sugar
2 tablespoons milk
1 teaspoon vanilla extract
1/2 cup creamy peanut butter
1 (12 ounce) jar hot fudge topping

Directions

Preheat oven to 350 degrees F (175 degrees C). Grease and flour 2 (9 inch) pans. Sift together the flour, baking powder and salt. Set aside.

In a large bowl, cream together the butter and sugar until light and fluffy. Beat in the eggs one at a time, then stir in the peanut butter and vanilla. Beat in the flour mixture alternately with the milk. Pour batter into prepared pans.

Bake in the preheated oven for 25 to 30 minutes, or until a toothpick inserted into the center of the cake comes out clean. Let cool in pans for 10 minutes, then turn out onto a wire rack and cool completely.

Make the Frosting and Filling: In a large bowl, beat 3/4 cup butter until smooth. Slowly beat in confectioners' sugar until smooth. Blend in 2 tablespoons milk and vanilla. Beat at high speed until light and fluffy. For filling, combine 1/2 cup of butter mixture with 1/2 cup peanut butter. For frosting, beat 1/2 cup of the (cool) hot fudge into remaining butter mixture.

To assemble: Place one cake layer on serving plate. Spread top with peanut butter filling. Place second layer on top and frost top and sides with fudge frosting. Warm the remaining fudge sauce and drizzle over cake when serving.

Vaselopita - Greek New Years Cake

Ingredients

1 cup butter
2 cups white sugar
3 cups all-purpose flour
6 eggs
2 teaspoons baking powder
1 cup warm milk (110 degrees F/45 degrees C)
1/2 teaspoon baking soda
1 tablespoon fresh lemon juice
1/4 cup blanched slivered almonds
2 tablespoons white sugar

Directions

Preheat oven to 350 degrees F (175 degrees C). Generously grease a 10 inch round cake pan.

In a medium bowl, cream the butter and sugar together until light. Stir in the flour and mix until the mixture is mealy. Add the eggs one at a time, mixing well after each addition. Combine the baking powder and milk, add to the egg mixture, mix well. Then combine the lemon juice and baking soda, stir into the batter. Pour into the prepared cake pan.

Bake for 20 minutes in the preheated oven. Remove and sprinkle the nuts and sugar over the cake, then return it to the oven for 20 to 30 additional minutes, until cake springs back to the touch. Gently cut a small hole in the cake and place a quarter in the hole. Try to cover the hole with sugar. Cool cake on a rack for 10 minutes before inverting onto a plate.

Serve cake warm. Each person in the family gets a slice starting with the youngest. The person who gets the quarter in their piece, gets good luck for the whole year!

Vodka Mocha Bundt Cake

Ingredients

1 (18.25 ounce) package yellow cake mix
1/4 cup white sugar
1 (5.9 ounce) package instant chocolate pudding mix
1 cup vegetable oil
4 eggs
1/4 cup vodka
1/4 cup coffee flavored liqueur
3/4 cup water

1/4 cup coffee flavored liqueur
1/4 cup confectioners' sugar

Directions

Preheat oven to 350 degrees F (175 degrees C). Grease and flour a 10 inch Bundt pan.

In a large bowl, combine Cake mix, sugar, pudding mix, oil, eggs, vodka, coffee liqueur and water. Mix at low speed for 1 minute and then at medium speed for 4 minutes.

Pour into prepared Bundt pan. Bake at 350 degrees F (175 degrees C) for one hour or until toothpick inserted into middle comes out clean. Cool for 10 minutes in the pan, then turn out onto wire rack.

To make the glaze: In a medium bowl, combine 1/4 cup coffee liqueur with the confectioners sugar. Mix well and pour over cake.

English Caraway Cake

Ingredients

1 tablespoon butter, softened
1/2 cup butter, softened
2 1/2 cups all-purpose flour
1 teaspoon baking powder
salt to taste
3/4 cup white sugar
1 tablespoon caraway seed
1 egg
1/2 cup milk

Directions

Preheat oven to 350 degrees F (175 degrees C). Grease and flour the bottom and sides of an 8 inch round cake pan with 1 tablespoon softened butter or margarine.

Sift together flour, salt, and baking powder.

Cream 1/2 cup butter or margarine and sugar together. Mix in caraway seeds and egg. Add flour mixture and milk, beating well. Pour batter into prepared cake pan.

Bake for about 45 minutes, or until a knife inserted into the center comes out clean. Cool.

Pink Azalea Cake

Ingredients

1 cup shortening
2 cups white sugar
1 1/3 cups milk
2 teaspoons vanilla extract
3 cups cake flour
4 teaspoons baking powder
1 teaspoon salt
6 egg whites
2 drops red food coloring

1 recipe Seven Minute Frosting
1/4 cup chopped maraschino cherries
1/4 cup chopped walnuts
2 drops red food coloring

Directions

Preheat oven to 350 degrees F (175 degrees C). Grease and flour 2 (9 inch) pans. Sift together the flour, baking powder, and salt. Set aside.

In a large bowl, cream together the shortening and sugar until light and fluffy. Beat in the flour mixture alternately with the milk and vanilla.

In a large glass or metal mixing bowl, beat egg whites until stiff peaks form. Fold 1/3 of the whites into the batter, then quickly fold in remaining whites until no streaks remain. Pour half of batter into one pan. Tint remaining batter pink with red food coloring, then pour into pan.

Bake in the preheated oven for 30 to 35 minutes, or until a toothpick inserted into the center of the cake comes out clean. Allow to cool.

Assemble the cake: In a medium bowl, tint half of the frosting pink with red food coloring. To remaining frosting, stir in cherries and nuts. Spread this filling between the layers. Frost top and sides with pink frosting.

Carolina Fish Cakes

Ingredients

3 cups water
2 potatoes, peeled
1/3 cup minced onion
1/3 cup chopped green bell pepper
1/3 cup red bell pepper, chopped
1/3 cup chopped celery
2 tablespoons butter
3 1/2 cups cooked cod, boned and flaked
4 tablespoons all-purpose flour
2 tablespoons grated Parmesan cheese
1 teaspoon Old Bay Seasoning TM
1/4 teaspoon mustard powder
1/2 teaspoon salt
ground black pepper to taste
1/2 cup milk
1/2 cup dry bread crumbs

Directions

Preheat oven to 400 degrees F (200 degrees C). Grease two baking sheets. Bring 3 cups of water to a boil. Add potatoes and cook until tender but still firm, about 15 minutes. Drain and mash. Reserve 1 cup mashed potatoes; discard remainder.

In a large saucepan, saute onion, green and red bell pepper and celery in butter over medium high heat until tender. Turn heat to low and fold in flaked fish. Slowly mix in flour, cheese, Old Bay seasoning, dry mustard, salt, pepper, mashed potatoes and milk. Mix gently but thoroughly. Remove pan from heat.

With floured hands shape batter into cakes 1/2 inch by 3 inches. Coat with breadcrumbs.

If you are baking the fish cakes bake them for 10 minutes, flip the cakes and bake another 15 minutes until golden brown.

Berry Tiramisu Cake

Ingredients

4 cups Assorted fresh berries
1 cup sugar
1 tablespoon lemon juice
2 teaspoons cornstarch
SPONGE CAKE:
1 1/2 cups all-purpose flour
1 1/8 cups sugar, divided
2 teaspoons baking powder
1/2 teaspoon salt
4 eggs, separated
1/2 cup water
1/3 cup vegetable oil
CREAM FILLING:
1 (8 ounce) package cream cheese, softened
1/2 cup confectioners' sugar
2 cups whipping cream, whipped

Directions

In a bowl, combine berries, sugar and lemon juice. Cover and refrigerate for 1 hour. Gently press berries; drain, reserving juice. Set berries aside. In a large saucepan, combine cornstarch and reserved juice until smooth. Bring to a boil; cook and stir for 1-2 minutes or until thickened. Cool completely.

In a large mixing bowl, combine the flour, 1 cup sugar, baking powder and salt. Whisk egg yolks, water and oil; add to dry ingredients, beating until smooth. In another mixing bowl, beat egg whites on medium speed until soft peaks form. Gradually add remaining sugar, beating on high until stiff peaks form; fold into batter. Spread into an ungreased 9-in. springform pan. Bake at 325 degrees F for 30-38 minutes or until cake springs back when lightly touched. Cool for 10 minutes; remove from pan and cool on a wire rack.

In a mixing bowl, beat cream cheese and confectioners' sugar until smooth. Fold in whipped cream. Split cake into three layers; place one layer on a serving plate. Spread with a third of the filling; top with a third of the berries and drizzle with 1/4 cup berry syrup. Refrigerate for at least 2 hours before serving.

Deep-Dish Cheesecake Coffee Cake

Ingredients

3 cups buttermilk baking mix
1/4 cup white sugar
1/4 cup butter, melted
1/2 cup milk

1/2 cup white sugar
1/2 teaspoon vanilla extract
2 eggs
1 (8 ounce) package cream cheese, softened
1/4 cup strawberry, apricot or raspberry preserves

Directions

Preheat oven to 375 degrees F (190 degrees C).

To make the crust, in a medium bowl, combine the baking mix, 1/4 cup sugar, melted butter and milk. Stir until a dough forms, then turn the dough out onto a clean surface that has been dusted with some baking mix. Knead for 30 turns. Pat the dough into the bottom and up the sides of an ungreased 9 inch round cake pan. In the same bowl, beat together the remaining 1/2 cup sugar, vanilla, eggs and cream cheese. Pour over the dough in the pan.

Bake for 30 minutes in the preheated oven, until the edges are golden and the filling is set. Allow the coffee cake to cool for 10 minutes, then spread the fruit preserves over the top.

Rippled Coffee Cake

Ingredients

1 (18.25 ounce) package yellow cake mix
1 cup sour cream
4 eggs
2/3 cup vegetable oil
1 cup packed brown sugar
1 tablespoon ground cinnamon
ICING:
2 cups confectioners' sugar
1/4 cup milk
2 teaspoons vanilla extract

Directions

In a mixing bowl, combine dry cake mix, sour cream, eggs and oil; beat well. Spread half of the batter into a greased 13-in. x 9-in. x 2-in. baking pan. Combine brown sugar and cinnamon; sprinkle over batter. Carefully spread remaining batter on top. bake at 350 degrees F for 30-35 minutes or until a toothpick inserted near the center comes out clean. Combine icing ingredients and drizzle over warm cake.

Mother's Day Pound Cake

Ingredients

1 teaspoon butter
1 cup butter
1 1/3 cups white sugar
2 teaspoons vanilla extract
4 eggs
1/4 teaspoon salt
1 lemon, zested
4 2/3 cups sifted all purpose flour
2 teaspoons baking powder
1/2 cup milk

Directions

Preheat oven to 350 degrees F (175 degrees C). Grease a 9 1/2-inch square baking pan with 1 teaspoon butter and set aside.

Melt 1 cup butter in a saucepan over low heat; stir in the sugar until thoroughly combined. Stir in the vanilla. Whisk in the eggs, one by one, whisking well between each egg. Stir in the salt and lemon zest. Transfer to a large mixing bowl.

In a separate bowl, sift the flour and baking powder together. Gently stir the flour mixture into the egg mixture. Stir in the milk, folding the batter lightly with a spatula until thoroughly combined. Pour the batter into the prepared baking pan.

Bake in the preheated oven until a toothpick inserted near the center of the cake comes out clean, 50 to 60 minutes. Let cool in pan on a wire rack for 10 minutes; invert the cake onto a second wire rack and let cool completely.

Sauerkraut Surprise Cake

Ingredients

1/2 cup butter
1 1/2 cups white sugar
3 eggs
1 teaspoon vanilla extract
2 cups all-purpose flour
1 teaspoon baking powder
1 teaspoon baking soda
1/2 teaspoon salt
1/2 cup unsweetened cocoa powder
1 cup water
1 cup drained and chopped sauerkraut
16 ounces semisweet chocolate chips
4 tablespoons butter
1/2 cup sour cream
2 3/4 cups confectioners' sugar

Directions

Preheat oven to 350 degrees F (175 degrees C). Grease and flour one 13x9 inch cake pan.

In a large mixing bowl, cream 1/2 cup butter or margarine and sugar until light. Beat in eggs, one at a time; add 1 teaspoon vanilla.

Sift together flour, baking powder, baking soda, 1/4 teaspoon salt and cocoa powder. Add to creamed mixture alternately with water, beating after each addition. Stir in sauerkraut. Pour batter into prepared pan.

Bake at 350 degrees F (175 degrees C) for 35 to 40 minutes. Let cake cool in pan. Frost with Sour Cream Chocolate Frosting. Cut into squares to serve.

To Make Sour Cream Chocolate Frosting: Melt the semi-sweet chocolate pieces and 4 T butter or margarine over low heat. Remove from heat. Blend in the sour cream, 1 teaspoon vanilla, and 1/4 teaspoon salt. Gradually add sifted confectioners' sugar to make spreading consistency. Beat well. Spread over cooled cake.

Chocolate Covered Gingerbread Cake

Ingredients

6 tablespoons butter, melted
3/4 cup packed brown sugar
1/3 cup molasses
2 eggs
1 tablespoon grated fresh ginger
1 3/4 cups all-purpose flour
2 teaspoons ground ginger
1 teaspoon baking powder
1 teaspoon ground cinnamon
1/2 teaspoon baking soda
1/4 teaspoon salt
1/4 teaspoon ground cloves
1 cup warm water
GLAZE:
1/2 cup heavy whipping cream
1/4 cup butter
2 tablespoons light corn syrup
8 (1 ounce) squares semisweet
chocolate, chopped
1 teaspoon vanilla extract

Directions

In a large mixing bowl, combine the butter, brown sugar, molasses, eggs and gingerroot. Combine the flour, ground ginger, baking powder, cinnamon, baking soda, salt and cloves; add to the molasses mixture alternately with water, beating just until combined.

Pour into a greased 13-in. x 9-in. x 2-in. baking pan. Bake at 350 degrees F for 25-30 minutes or until a toothpick inserted near the center of cake comes out clean. Cool for 10 minutes before removing from pan to a wire rack to cool completely.

In a medium saucepan, combine the cream, butter and corn syrup; bring to a simmer over medium heat. Remove from the heat. Stir in chocolate and vanilla until smooth. Let stand until cool but still pourable, about 20 minutes.

Place a baking sheet underneath the wire rack. Reserve 1/2 cup glaze. Pour remaining glaze over cake; spreading with spatula cover top and sides. Chill cake and reserved glaze until glaze is just firm enough to pipe, about 1 hour.

Pipe reserved glaze in a decorative pattern over cake. Cover and refrigerate. Remove from refrigerator 30 minutes before serving.

Treasure Chest Cake

Ingredients

1 large orange
1 cup raisins
1 cup walnuts
1/2 cup shortening
1 cup white sugar
1 cup buttermilk
1 egg
2 cups all-purpose flour
3/4 teaspoon baking soda
1 teaspoon baking powder
1/4 teaspoon salt
1/4 teaspoon ground cinnamon
1/4 teaspoon ground cloves
1/4 teaspoon ground allspice
4 tablespoons heavy whipping cream
1 teaspoon vanilla extract
3 cups confectioners' sugar
1 tablespoon orange zest

Directions

Squeeze the juice from the orange, and then remove the white from the peel. Place the peel, nuts and raisins in a food processor, and grind coarsely. Add the orange juice to the nut mixture.

Cream the shortening and sugar together until light and fluffy. Beat the egg, and add it to the creamed mixture.

Sift together the flour, soda, baking powder, and spices. Add the flour mixture alternately with the buttermilk to the creamed mixture. Stir in 3/4 of the nut mixture, and reserve the rest for the icing.

Pour batter into a greased and floured 10 inch square pan. Bake at 350 degrees F (175 degrees C) for about 1 hour. Cool.

To Make Frosting: Blend the cream and vanilla with the confectioners' sugar in a small mixing bowl. Add the remaining nut mixture and the grated orange rind. Frost the cooled cake with this icing.

Sour Cream Coffee Cake

Ingredients

1/2 cup butter, softened
1 cup sugar
2 eggs
1 cup sour cream
1 teaspoon vanilla extract
2 cups all-purpose flour
1 teaspoon baking powder
1 teaspoon baking soda
1/4 teaspoon salt
TOPPING:
1/4 cup sugar
1/3 cup packed brown sugar
2 teaspoons ground cinnamon
1/2 cup chopped pecans

Directions

In a mixing bowl, cream butter and sugar. Add eggs, sour cream and vanilla; mix well. Combine flour, baking powder, baking soda and salt; add to creamed mixture and beat until combined. Pour half the batter into a greased 13-in. x 9-in. baking pan. Combine topping ingredients; sprinkle half of topping over batter. Add remaining batter and topping. Bake at 325 degrees F for 40 minutes or until done.

Crazy Chocolate Cake

Ingredients

3 cups all-purpose flour
2 cups white sugar
5/8 cup unsweetened cocoa powder
1 teaspoon salt
2 teaspoons baking soda
1 teaspoon vanilla extract
2 cups cold water
2 teaspoons distilled white vinegar
2/3 cup vegetable oil

Directions

Mix all ingredients right in a 9 x 13 inch pan.

Bake at 350 degrees F (175 degrees C) for 35 minutes. Remove from oven and cool. Frost with your favorite frosting.

White Chocolate Amaretto Cake

Ingredients

1 (18.25 ounce) package yellow cake mix
4 eggs
1 (3.3 ounce) package instant white chocolate pudding mix
1/2 cup cold water
1/2 cup vegetable oil
1/2 cup amaretto liqueur
1/4 teaspoon almond extract

1/2 cup butter
1/4 cup water
1 cup white sugar
1/2 cup amaretto liqueur

1 (16 ounce) package vanilla frosting
1/4 cup blanched slivered almonds

Directions

Preheat oven to 350 degrees F (175 degrees C). Lightly oil a 10 inch non-stick Bundt pan.

In a large bowl, combine cake mix, eggs, pudding mix, 1/2 cup of cold water, oil, 1/2 cup amaretto and 1/4 teaspoon almond extract. Blend well for approximately 3 minutes.

Pour batter into prepared 10 inch Bundt pan. Bake at 350 degrees F (175 degrees C) for 45 minutes to an hour, or until a toothpick inserted into the center of the cake comes out clean.

Remove cake from oven, and use an ice pick or skewer to make as many holes as possible into the cake. Apply glaze while cake is still warm. Slowly and patiently drizzle glaze over cake, including the edges and center of Bundt pan. Allow cake to cool in the pan for at least 2 hours.

To make the glaze: Combine butter, sugar, 1/4 cup water, and 1/2 cup amaretto in a saucepan. Bring to a boil, and continue to boil for 10 minutes, stirring constantly.

Topping: Lightly toast slivered almonds in the oven. This will take 5 to 10 minutes. Stir frequently and be careful not to burn. Heat 1/4 cup of the prepared frosting in the microwave for 10 seconds, to soften. Place the cake on serving dish and use a spoon to drizzle the softened frosting over the cake. Scatter toasted almonds over cake before frosting cools.

Lemon Yogurt Pound Cake with Lemon Glaze

Ingredients

2 1/4 cups sifted all-purpose flour
1 1/4 cups sugar
1 teaspoon salt
1/2 teaspoon baking soda
1 1/2 teaspoons grated lemon peel
1 teaspoon vanilla extract
1 cup CRISCO® Shortening
1 (8 ounce) container lemon yogurt
3 eggs

Lemon Glaze
1 lemon, juiced
1 cup Confectioners' sugar

Directions

Preheat oven to 325 degrees. Grease a 10-inch tube (or bundt) pan with CRISCO® Shortening. Dust lightly with flour; set aside.

In the bowl of an electric mixer, combine all ingredients low speed. Beat for 3 minutes at medium speed. Pour batter into prepared pan.

Bake 50 to 60 minutes or until toothpick inserted in center comes out clean.

In a small bowl, combine lemon juice and confectioners' sugar until smooth. Brush over warm cake. (The glaze will be thin and absorbed into cake.)

King Cake

Ingredients

2 (.25 ounce) packages active dry yeast
1/2 cup white sugar
1 cup warm milk (110 degrees F/45 degrees C)
1/2 cup butter, melted
5 egg yolks
4 cups all-purpose flour
2 teaspoons salt
1 teaspoon ground nutmeg
1 teaspoon grated lemon zest

1 (8 ounce) package cream cheese
1/2 cup confectioners' sugar

2 cups confectioners' sugar
1/4 cup lemon juice
2 tablespoons milk
1 tablespoon multicolored candy sprinkles

Directions

In a large bowl, dissolve yeast and white sugar in warm milk. Let stand until creamy, about 10 minutes.

Stir the egg yolks and melted butter into the milk mixture. In a separate bowl, combine the flour, salt, nutmeg and lemon zest. Beat the flour mixture into the milk/egg mixture 1 cup at a time. When the dough has pulled together, turn it out onto a lightly floured surface and knead until smooth and supple, about 8 minutes. Lightly oil a large bowl, place the dough in the bowl and turn to coat with oil. Cover with a damp cloth and let rise in a warm place until doubled in volume, about 2 hours.

In a small bowl, combine the cream cheese and 1/2 cup confectioners' sugar. Mix well. In another small bowl, combine the remaining 2 cups confectioners' sugar, lemon juice and 2 tablespoons milk. Mix well and set aside.

Turn the dough out onto a floured surface. Roll the dough out into a 6x30 inch rectangle. Spread the cream cheese filling across the center of the dough. Bring the two long edges together and seal completely. Using your hands shape the dough into a long cylinder and place on a greased baking sheet, seam-side down. Shape the dough into a ring press the baby into the ring from the bottom so that it is completely hidden by the dough. Place a well-greased 2 pound metal coffee can the center of the ring to maintain the shape during baking. Cover the ring with a towel and place in a warm place to rise until doubled in size, about 45 minutes. Meanwhile, preheat oven to 350 degrees F (175 degrees C).

Bake in preheated oven until golden brown, about 30 minutes. Remove the coffee can and allow the bread to cool. Drizzle cooled cake with lemon/sugar glaze and decorate with candy sprinkles.

Pastel Pound Cake

Ingredients

1 cup butter, softened
2 cups sugar
4 eggs
1 teaspoon almond extract
1 teaspoon vanilla extract
3 cups all-purpose flour
3/4 teaspoon salt
1/2 teaspoon baking powder
1/2 teaspoon baking soda
1 cup buttermilk
1 cup rainbow colored miniature marshmallows
confectioners' sugar

Directions

In a large mixing bowl, cream butter and sugar. Add eggs, one at a time, beating after each addition. Add extracts. Combine the flour, salt, baking powder and baking soda; add to creamed mixture alternately with buttermilk, beating well after each addition.

Pour half of the batter into a greased and floured 10-in. fluted tube pan. Sprinkle with marshmallows. Top with remaining batter. Bake at 350 degrees F for 55-60 minutes or until a toothpick inserted near the center comes out clean.

Cool for 10 minutes before removing from pan to a wire rack to cool completely. Dust with confectioners' sugar.

Caramel Nougat Cake III

Ingredients

4 (2.1 ounce) bars milk chocolate covered caramel and nougat candy
1 cup unsalted butter
2 cups white sugar
4 eggs
1 cup buttermilk
2 1/2 cups all-purpose flour
1/4 teaspoon baking soda
2 teaspoons vanilla extract
1 cup chopped pecans

Directions

Preheat oven to 350 degrees F (175 degrees C). Lightly grease and flour one 10 inch bundt pan.

Melt candy bars and 1/2 cup of the butter or margarine in the top half of a double boiler. Let cool.

Cream remaining 1/2 cup butter or margarine with the sugar. Add eggs one at a time mixing well after each one. Add buttermilk alternately with flour and soda to egg mixture. Add vanilla and melted candy mixture and mix until smooth. Fold in chopped pecans and pour into the prepared pan.

Bake at 350 degrees (175 degrees C) for one hour. Cool for 15 minutes in the pan then turn out onto wire rack to cool.

Heavenly Angel Food Cake

Ingredients

12 eggs
1 1/4 cups confectioners' sugar
1 cup all-purpose flour
1 1/2 teaspoons cream of tartar
1 1/2 teaspoons vanilla extract
1/2 teaspoon almond extract
1/4 teaspoon salt
1 cup sugar

Directions

Separate eggs; discard yolks or refrigerate for another use. Measure egg whites, adding or removing whites as needed to equal 1-1/2 cups. Place in a mixing bowl; let stand at room temperature for 30 minutes.

Meanwhile, sift confectioners' sugar and flour together three times; set aside. Add cream of tartar, extracts and salt to egg whites; beat on high speed. Gradually add sugar, beating until sugar is dissolved and stiff peaks form. Fold in flour mixture, 1/4 cup at a time. Gently spoon into an ungreased 10-in. tube pan. Cut through batter with a knife to remove air pockets. Bake at 350 degrees F for 40-45
minutes or until cake springs back when lightly touched.
Immediately invert pan; cool completely before removing cake from pan.

Quick Sunshine Cake

Ingredients

1 (18.25 ounce) package moist yellow cake mix
4 eggs
1/2 cup vegetable oil
1 (11 ounce) can mandarin oranges, juice reserved
1 (16 ounce) package frozen whipped topping, thawed
1 (5 ounce) package instant vanilla pudding mix
1 (20 ounce) can crushed pineapple with juice

Directions

Beat the eggs, and add them to the boxed cake mix. Add the oil and the mandarine oranges to the batter; remember to add the juice as well as the fruit. Pour the batter into a greased and floured 9 x 13 inch pan.

Bake the cake for 40 minutes in a preheated oven at 325 degrees F (165 degrees C). Cool on wire rack.

While cake is baking, prepare the frosting by mixing together the whipped dessert topping, the package of instant pudding, and the crushed pineapple with its juices. Set frosting in refrigerator to set. Frost when cake has thoroughly cooled.

Chinese New Year Turnip Cake

Ingredients

2 tablespoons vegetable oil
8 ounces Chinese dried mushrooms, soaked overnight in water
1/3 cup dried shrimp, soaked in water overnight and drained
1 pound pork sausage, sliced
1 tablespoon vegetable oil
2 slices fresh ginger root
3 turnips, shredded
1 1/2 teaspoons Chinese five-spice powder
2 teaspoons salt
1/2 teaspoon chicken bouillon granules
1 tablespoon ground white pepper
2/3 pound white rice flour

Directions

Heat 2 tablespoons oil in a wok or large skillet over high heat. Add mushrooms, shrimp and sausages and saute for 1/2 minute. Remove from skillet and set aside. Heat 1 more tablespoon oil in wok/skillet. Add ginger and saute a bit. Add shredded turnips and stir fry for about 3 minutes (do NOT remove turnip water). Add 5-spice powder, salt, chicken bouillon and white pepper and toss all together until evenly distributed. Extract ginger slices from mixture.

Turn off heat. Top turnip mixture with rice flour and use chopsticks to toss and mix flour in evenly. Add reserved sausage mixture and toss to mix in. Remove mixture from wok/skillet and place into a 9x2 inch deep round cake pan.

Clean wok/skillet, fill with water and bring to a boil. Place cake pan on a round wire rack over boiling water. Reduce heat to low and let simmer, steaming cake 'batter', for 45 minutes. (Note: you can also use a large bamboo steamer if you have one). When 'cake' is steamed through, slice into pieces and serve hot OR cool on wire rack before covering tightly with plastic wrap and placing in refrigerator to chill.

Toasted Angel Food Cake

Ingredients

1 tablespoon cream cheese, softened
2 angel food cake
1 teaspoon raspberry preserves
2 teaspoons butter or margarine, softened
confectioners' sugar

Directions

Spread cream cheese on one slice of cake; spread preserves on second slice. Place slices together, sandwich-style. Spread butter on outsides of cake. In a skillet over medium heat, toast cake on both sides until lightly browned and cream cheese is melted. Dust with confectioners' sugar. Serve immediately.

Easy German Chocolate Cake

Ingredients

1 1/3 cups flaked coconut
1 cup chopped pecans
1 (18.25 ounce) package German chocolate cake mix
1 (8 ounce) package cream cheese, softened
1/2 cup butter or margarine, softened
1 egg
4 cups confectioners' sugar

Directions

Sprinkle the coconut and pecans into a greased and floured 13-in. x 9-in. x 2-in. baking pan.

Prepare cake mix according to package directions. Pour batter into prepared pan.

In a mixing bowl, beat cream cheese and butter until smooth. Add egg and sugar; beat until smooth. Drop by tablespoonfuls over the batter. Carefully spread to within 1 in. of edges.

Bake at 325 degrees for 55-60 minutes or until a toothpick inserted near the center comes out clean. Cool for 10 minutes; invert onto a serving plate.

Chewy Butter Cake

Ingredients

1 (18.25 ounce) package yellow cake mix
1/2 cup margarine, softened
3 eggs
4 teaspoons vanilla extract
1 (8 ounce) package cream cheese
4 cups confectioners' sugar

Directions

Preheat oven to 350 degrees F (175 degrees C). Grease and flour a 9x13 inch pan.

In a large bowl, combine cake mix, margarine, 1 egg and 2 teaspoons vanilla. Press into a 9x13 inch pan.

Using the same bowl, combine cream cheese, 2 eggs, 2 teaspoons vanilla and 4 cups confectioners' sugar. Mix together until smooth. Pour over cake mixture.

Bake in the preheated oven for 35 to 40 minutes. Cake will rise up around sides of pan and look fallen when done. Allow to cool.

Dirt Cake II

Ingredients

1 (20 ounce) package chocolate sandwich cookies with creme filling
1/4 cup butter, softened
1 (8 ounce) package cream cheese, softened
1 cup confectioners' sugar
1 teaspoon vanilla extract
2 (3.9 ounce) packages instant chocolate pudding mix
3 cups milk
1 (12 ounce) container frozen whipped topping, thawed
15 gummi worms

Directions

Put the cookies in a food processor and process until they become fine crumbs. Set aside.

In a large bowl, combine the butter or margarine, cream cheese, confectioners sugar and vanilla flavoring. Beat on low speed to mix then beat on medium speed until smooth. Add the chocolate pudding mix and milk to the bowl. Beat on low speed to combine.

Fold the whipped topping into the pudding mixture with a rubber spatula.

Assemble in the ungreased 9x13 inch pan in layers as follows: first layer, 1/3 cookie crumbs; second layer, 1/2 pudding mixture; third layer, 1/3 cookie crumbs; fifth layer, 1/3 cookie crumbs.

Tuck the ends of gummy worms in the cookie "dirt". Be sure to have a worm on each piece. Store in the refrigerator. Chill for at least 3 hours before serving. Cut into 15 squares, or serve with a clean garden trowel or a toy sand shovel if serving in the flower pot.

Pound Cake with Rum Topping

Ingredients

3 1/2 cups all-purpose flour
1 teaspoon baking powder
1 cup butter
3 3/4 cups confectioners' sugar
4 eggs
2 teaspoons vanilla extract
1 cup cold water

1 cup white sugar
1/4 cup water
1/2 cup butter
5 tablespoons rum

Directions

Preheat oven to 350 degrees F (175 degrees C). Grease and flour a 10 inch tube pan. Sift together the flour and baking powder; set aside.

In a large bowl, cream together the butter and confectioners' sugar until light and fluffy. Beat in the eggs one at a time, then stir in the vanilla. Beat in the flour mixture alternately with 1 cup water, mixing just until incorporated. Spread into prepared pan.

Bake in the preheated oven for 60 to 70 minutes, or until a toothpick inserted into the center of the cake comes out clean.

In a small saucepan over medium heat, combine 1 cup sugar, 1/4 cup water, and 1/2 cup butter. Bring to a boil, stirring until sugar is dissolved. Remove from heat, and stir in rum. Pour hot syrup over hot cake. Let soak for 20 minutes.

Moist Carrot Cake

Ingredients

1/2 cup shortening
1 cup sugar
1 (10.75 ounce) can condensed tomato soup, undiluted
1 egg
2 cups all-purpose flour
1 1/2 teaspoons baking soda
1 teaspoon ground cinnamon
Dash salt
1 cup shredded carrots
1/2 cup chopped walnuts
1/2 cup raisins or dried currants (optional)
FROSTING:
1 (8 ounce) package cream cheese, softened
3 cups confectioners' sugar
1 teaspoon vanilla extract
1 tablespoon milk
Chopped walnuts

Directions

In a large mixing bowl, cream shortening and sugar. Add soup and egg; mix well. Combine flour, baking soda, cinnamon and salt; beat into creamed mixture. Stir in the carrots, walnuts and raisins or currants if desired. Pour into a greased 10-in. fluted tube pan. Bake at 350 degrees F for 45-50 minutes or until cake tests done. Cool in pan 10 minutes before removing to a wire rack to cool completely.

In another mixing bowl, combine the first four frosting ingredients; beat until smooth. Frost cake; top with walnuts if desired.

Red Velvet Cake V

Ingredients

1 cup butter
1/2 cup shortening
3 cups white sugar
5 eggs
3 cups all-purpose flour
1/2 cup unsweetened cocoa powder
1/2 teaspoon baking powder
1 cup milk
2 ounces red food coloring
1 teaspoon vanilla extract

Directions

Preheat oven to 325 degrees F (165 degrees C). Grease and flour a 10 inch Bundt pan. Sift together the flour, cocoa and baking powder; set aside.

In a large bowl, cream together the butter, shortening and sugar until light and fluffy. Add the eggs one at a time, beating well with each addition. Add the flour mixture alternately with the milk. Mix well then stir in the vanilla and red food coloring.

Pour batter into a 10 inch Bundt pan. Bake for 60 to 90 minutes in the preheated oven, or until a toothpick inserted into the cake comes out clean.

Sweet Corn Cake

Ingredients

1/2 cup butter, softened
1/3 cup masa harina
1/4 cup water
1 1/2 cups frozen whole-kernel corn, thawed
1/4 cup cornmeal
1/3 cup white sugar
2 tablespoons heavy whipping cream
1/4 teaspoon salt
1/2 teaspoon baking powder

Directions

In a medium bowl beat butter until it is creamy. Add the Mexican corn flour and water and beat until well mixed.

Using a food processor, process thawed corn, but leave chunky. Stir into the butter mixture.

In a separate bowl, mix cornmeal, sugar, cream, salt, and baking powder. Add to corn flour mixture and stir to combine. Pour batter into an ungreased 8x8 inch baking pan. Smooth batter and cover with aluminum foil. Place pan into a 9x13 inch baking dish that is filled a third of the way with water.

Bake in a preheated 350 degree oven F (175 degrees C) oven for 50 to 60 minutes. Allow to cool for 10 minutes. Use an ice cream scoop for easy removal from pan.

Luscious Date Bar Cake

Ingredients

1 cup all-purpose flour
1 teaspoon baking powder
1 pinch salt
1 cup brown sugar
3 eggs, beaten
1/2 teaspoon vanilla extract
1 1/2 cups chopped pecans
2 cups chopped dates

Directions

Preheat oven to 325 degrees F (165 degrees C). Grease and flour a 9x13 inch pan. Sift together the flour, baking powder and salt. Set aside.

In a large bowl, cream together the sugar and eggs, then stir in the flour mixture. Stir in the vanilla, pecans and dates.

Pour batter into prepared pan. Bake in the preheated oven for 35 minutes, or until a toothpick inserted into the center of the cake comes out clean. Cut into bars while cake is still warm.

Pistachio Nut Cake II

Ingredients

1 (18.25 ounce) package yellow cake mix
2 (3.4 ounce) packages instant pistachio pudding mix
1 cup vegetable oil
3 eggs
1 cup carbonated water
1/2 cup chopped pistachio nuts
1 (1.5 ounce) envelope instant dessert topping
1 1/2 cups milk

Directions

Preheat oven to 350 degrees F (175 degrees C). Grease and flour a 10 inch Bundt pan.

In a medium bowl, stir together the cake mix and 1 package of instant pudding. Add the oil, eggs and club soda, mix well. Fold in the chopped nuts, reserving some for garnish if desired. Pour into the prepared pan.

Bake for 50 to 60 minutes in the preheated oven, until cake springs back when lightly touched. Cool for 10 minutes in the pan before inverting onto a wire rack to cool completely. In a medium bowl, stir together the instant whipped topping and instant pudding. Add the milk and mix until light and fluffy. Slice cooled cake into layers, fill and frost including the hole in the middle. Garnish with nuts if desired. Keep chilled until serving.

Lisa's Chocolate Chocolate Chip Cake

Ingredients

1 (18.25 ounce) package chocolate cake mix
1 (3.9 ounce) package instant chocolate pudding mix
1 cup vegetable oil
4 eggs
1/2 cup hot water
1 cup sour cream
1 teaspoon vanilla extract
1 cup mini semi-sweet chocolate chips

Directions

Preheat oven to 350 degrees F (175 degrees C). Grease and flour a Bundt pan.

Combine cake mix, pudding mix, oil, eggs, water, sour cream, and vanilla. Beat until smooth. Stir in chocolate chips. Pour batter into prepared pan.

Bake for 1 hour. Allow to cool.

Chocolate Angel Food Cake I

Ingredients

2 cups egg whites
1/4 teaspoon salt
1 1/4 teaspoons cream of tartar
1 1/4 cups white sugar
1 1/4 cups confectioners' sugar
1 1/4 cups cake flour
1/4 cup unsweetened cocoa powder
1 1/4 teaspoons vanilla extract

Directions

Preheat oven to 325 degrees F (165 degrees C).

In a medium bowl, mix confectioners' sugar, cake flour, and cocoa. Sift together 2 times, and set aside.

In a clean large bowl, whip egg whites, salt, and cream of tartar with an electric mixer on high speed until very stiff. Fold in white sugar 2 tablespoons at a time while continuing to mix. Fold in flour mixture, a little at a time, until fully incorporated. Stir in vanilla. Pour into a 10 inch tube pan.

Bake at 325 degrees F (165 degrees C) for approximately 1 hour, or until cake springs back when touched.

Barbadian Plain Cake

Ingredients

1 1/2 cups white sugar
2 cups butter
4 1/2 teaspoons baking powder
3 cups all-purpose flour
4 eggs
1 tablespoon vanilla extract
1 tablespoon almond extract
2 cups milk

Directions

Preheat oven to 400 degrees F (205 degrees C). Lightly grease and flour one 9 or 10 inch bundt pan.

By hand with a spatula cream butter and sugar together until light and fluffy. Add eggs all at once and beat well.

Sift the flour and the baking powder together. Add to butter mixture along with 1 cup of the milk. Continue to beat well (the batter will be doughy). Add the remaining 1 cup of milk along with the vanilla, and almond extracts. Pour batter into the prepared pan.

Bake at 400 degrees F (205 degrees C) for 1 hour. Reduce heat to 350 degrees F (175 degrees C) and continue baking for 15 minutes longer.

Whipped Cream Cake I

Ingredients

1 cup heavy whipping cream
1 cup white sugar
2 eggs
1 1/2 cups cake flour
1/2 teaspoon salt
2 teaspoons baking powder
1 teaspoon vanilla extract

Directions

Sift and measure flour. Add salt and baking powder, and sift again.

Whip the cream until stiff. Drop in eggs one at a time, and beat until light and fluffy. Add sugar and vanilla, and beat again. Add sifted ingredients gradually to mixture; beat well after each addition. Pour batter into greased 9 inch round pan.

Bake at 350 degrees F (175 degrees C) for 35 minutes.

Apricot Coffee Cake

Ingredients

1 (.25 ounce) package active dry yeast
1/4 cup warm water (105 degrees to 115 degrees)
3/4 cup warm milk (110 to 115 degrees F)
1 egg
1/2 cup butter or margarine, softened
4 cups all-purpose flour
1/2 cup sugar
1/2 teaspoon salt
APRICOT FILLING:
12 ounces dried apricots
3/4 cup water
3/4 cup sugar
1/4 teaspoon ground cinnamon
GLAZE:
1/2 cup confectioners' sugar
1 teaspoon milk
1/2 teaspoon butter or margarine, softened
1/2 teaspoon vanilla extract

Directions

In a large mixing bowl, dissolve yeast in warm water. Add warm milk, egg and butter; mix. Add 2-1/2 cups flour, sugar and salt; beat until smooth. Add enough remaining flour to form a soft dough. Turn onto floured surface; knead until smooth and elastic, about 6-8 minutes. Place in a greased bowl, turning once to grease top. Cover and let rise in a warm place until doubled, about 1 hour. For filling, combine apricots and water in a saucepan. Cover and simmer for 30 minutes. Cool 10 minutes. Pour into a blender; process at high speed until smooth. Stir in sugar and cinnamon; set aside. Punch dough down. Divide in half and roll each half into a 15-in. x 12-in. rectangle. Place on a greased baking sheet. Spread half of the filling in a 15-in. x 4-in. strip down center of dough. With a sharp knife, cut dough on each side of apricot filling into 1-in. wide strips. Fold strips alternately across filling to give braided effect. Repeat with remaining dough and filling. Cover and let rise until doubled, about 30 minutes. Bake at 375 degrees F for 20 minutes or until golden brown. Cool on wire racks for 15 minutes. Combine glaze ingredients; drizzle over warm coffee cakes. Serve warm or allow to cool completely.

Lemon Polenta Cake

Ingredients

2 2/3 cups turbinado sugar
1 pound butter, room temperature
6 eggs, room temperature
5 cups almond meal
1 1/3 cups fine cornmeal
1 teaspoon baking powder
1/2 teaspoon salt
6 lemons, juiced and zested
3/4 cup superfine sugar

Directions

Preheat an oven to 300 degrees F (150 degrees C). Line the bottom of a 10-inch cake pan with parchment paper.

Beat the sugar and butter with an electric mixer until light and fluffy. The mixture should be noticeably lighter in color. Add the room-temperature eggs one at a time, allowing each egg to blend into the butter mixture before adding the next.

In a separate bowl, combine the almond meal, cornmeal, baking powder, salt, and lemon zest. Gently fold it into the butter mixture, stirring just until combined.

Pour the batter into the prepared pan and bake in the preheated oven until the cake is golden and a toothpick inserted into the center comes out clean, 90 to 120 minutes.

While the cake is baking, combine the lemon juice and superfine sugar in a saucepan. Bring to a boil over medium-high heat and boil until the sugar has dissolved and the liquid is reduced by half. Remove from heat.

Remove the cake from the oven and use a skewer or toothpick to prick holes in the cake. Pour the lemon syrup over the surface. Allow the cake to cool in the pan completely before serving.

White Texas Sheet Cake

Ingredients

1 cup butter
1 cup water
2 cups all-purpose flour
2 cups white sugar
2 eggs
1/2 cup sour cream
1 teaspoon almond extract
1/2 teaspoon salt
1 teaspoon baking soda
1/2 cup butter
1/4 cup milk
4 1/2 cups confectioners' sugar
1/2 teaspoon almond extract
1 cup chopped walnuts

Directions

In a large saucepan, bring 1 cup butter or margarine and water to a boil. Remove from heat, and stir in flour, sugar, eggs, sour cream, 1 teaspoon almond extract, salt, and baking soda until smooth. Pour batter into a greased 10 x 15 x 1 inch baking pan.

Bake at 375 degrees F (190 degrees C) for 20 to 22 minutes, or until cake is golden brown and tests done. Cool for 20 minutes.

Combine 1/2 cup butter or margarine and milk in a saucepan; bring to a boil. Remove from heat. Mix in sugar and 1/2 teaspoon almond extract. Stir in pecans. Spread frosting over warm cake.

Chocolate Cakes with Liquid Centers

Ingredients

1/2 cup butter
4 (1 ounce) squares bittersweet chocolate
2 eggs
2 egg yolks
1/4 cup white sugar
2 teaspoons all-purpose flour

Directions

Preheat oven to 450 degrees F (230 degrees C). Butter and flour four 4 ounce ramekins or custard cups.

In the top half of a double boiler set over simmering water, heat the butter and the chocolate until chocolate is almost completely melted.

Beat the eggs, egg yolks and sugar together until light colored and thick.

Beat together the melted chocolate and butter. While beating, slowly pour the chocolate mixture into the egg mixture, then quickly beat in the flour and mix until just combined.

Divide the batter between the four molds and bake at 450 degrees F (230 degrees C) for 6 to 7 minutes. The centers of the cakes will still be quite soft. Invert cakes on serving plates and let sit for about 15 seconds, then unmold. Serve immediately with fresh whipped cream, if desired.

Molasses Sponge Cake

Ingredients

5 egg whites
1/4 cup white sugar
1/2 teaspoon salt
5 egg yolks
1/4 cup white sugar
1/2 cup molasses
1 teaspoon lemon zest
2 teaspoons lemon juice
3/4 cup cake flour

Directions

Preheat oven to 350 degrees F (175 degrees C).

Beat egg whites to form moist peaks. Gradually beat in 1/4 cup white sugar and salt. Beat until very stiff and shiny.

Beat egg yolks and 1/4 cup white sugar together until very light and fluffy. Beat in molasses, grated lemon rind and lemon juice. Stir in cake flour. Fold meringue gently into batter. Pour batter into an ungreased 9 inch tube pan.

Bake for 45 minutes. Remove cake from oven, and invert until cool. Loosen edges, and remove cake from pan.

Easy Spiced Cake Mix Bars

Ingredients

1 (18.25 ounce) package yellow cake mix
1/2 teaspoon ground cinnamon
1/4 teaspoon ground cloves
1 egg
1/3 cup vegetable oil
1/3 cup applesauce
1/2 cup chopped walnuts
1/2 cup semisweet chocolate chips
1/4 cup dried currants, (optional)

Directions

Preheat oven to 350 degrees F (175 degrees C). Grease a 9x13 inch baking pan.

In a large bowl, stir together the cake mix, cinnamon and cloves. Add egg, oil and applesauce; mix well. Stir in the walnuts and chocolate chips. Mix in currants if desired. spread the mixture evenly into the prepared pan.

Bake for 30 to 35 minutes in the preheated oven, until lightly browned. Cool before cutting into bars.

Fruit Cocktail Cake

Ingredients

CAKE:
1 1/2 cups sugar
2 cups all-purpose flour
2 eggs
1 teaspoon vanilla extract
2 tablespoons lemon juice
2 teaspoons baking soda
3/4 teaspoon salt
1 (16 ounce) can fruit cocktail with syrup
TOPPING:
1/2 cup packed brown sugar
1/2 cup flaked coconut
SAUCE:
1/4 cup evaporated milk
3/4 cup sugar
1 teaspoon vanilla extract 1/2 cup butter or margarine 1/2 cup flaked coconut
1/2 cup chopped walnuts

Directions

In a large mixing bowl, combine all cake ingredients; mix well. Pour into a 13-in. x 9-in. x 2-in. pan and sprinkle with topping ingredients. Bake at 350 degrees F for 35-40 minutes. Meanwhile, combine all sauce ingredients in a medium saucepan and bring to a boil. When cake is done and still warm, pour sauce over cake. Cool to room temperature.

Ingredients

1 (18.25 ounce) package chocolate cake mix
3 cups heavy whipping cream
1/3 cup confectioners' sugar
1 (21 ounce) can cherry pie filling

Directions

Preheat oven according to box directions for cupcakes. Line cupcake pans with cupcake liners. (Be sure to use liners, and not just the pan.)

Mix cake according to package directions. Fill cupcake liners slightly less than half full. (You want the cupcake to bake up close to level with the top of the liner.

Bake according to package directions. Cool completely.

In chilled medium bowl combine whipping cream and sugar. Beat with an electric mixer on high until stiff peaks form. Refrigerate until ready to use.

After cupcakes are cooled completely, frost with a level layer of whipped cream frosting.

Spoon remaining frosting into pastry bag fitted with a star decorating tip. Pipe around the edges of the cupcakes.

Spoon a small amount of cherry pie filling in the center of each. Refrigerate and enjoy!

Cream Cake

Ingredients

2 eggs
3/4 cup white sugar
1 teaspoon vanilla extract
1 1/2 cups all-purpose flour
2 teaspoons baking powder
1 teaspoon salt
1 cup heavy whipping cream

Directions

Preheat oven to 350 degrees F (175 degrees C). Grease one 9x9 inch square pan.

Beat eggs in a small bowl until very thick. Add the sugar and the vanilla, beating well.

Combine the flour, baking powder, and salt. In three parts add the flour mixture alternately with the whipping cream to the egg mixture, beginning and ending with the flour mixture. Pour the batter into the prepared pan.

Bake at 350 degrees F (175 degrees C) for 30 to 40 minutes or until a toothpick inserted near the center comes out clean.

Graham Griddle Cakes

Ingredients

3/4 cup all-purpose flour
3/4 cup graham cracker crumbs
2 tablespoons brown sugar
2 teaspoons baking powder
1/4 teaspoon salt
1/2 cup chopped pecans
1 cup milk
2 tablespoons butter, melted
1 egg

Directions

In a large mixing bowl, combine flour, graham cracker crumbs, brown sugar, baking powder, salt and pecans (if desired). In a separate bowl, stir together milk, butter and egg. Add to the flour mixture and stir well.

Heat a lightly oiled griddle or frying pan over medium high heat. Pour or scoop the batter onto the griddle, using approximately 1/4 cup for each pancake. Brown on both sides and serve hot.

Poppy Seed Bundt Cake III

Ingredients

1 (18.25 ounce) package yellow cake mix
1 (3.4 ounce) package instant vanilla pudding mix
2 tablespoons poppy seeds
1 cup water
1/2 cup vegetable oil
4 eggs
1 teaspoon almond extract

Directions

Preheat oven to 350 degrees F (175 degrees C). Grease and flour a 10 inch Bundt pan.

In a large bowl, stir together cake mix, pudding mix and poppy seeds. Make a well in the center and pour in water, oil, and eggs. Beat on low speed until blended. Scrape bowl, and beat 4 minutes on medium speed. Pour batter into prepared pan.

Bake in the preheated oven for 50 minutes, or until a toothpick inserted into the center of the cake comes out clean. Let cool in pan for 10 minutes, then turn out onto a wire rack and cool completely.

Williamsburg Orange Cake

Ingredients

2 3/4 cups cake flour
1 1/2 cups white sugar
1 1/2 teaspoons baking soda
3/4 teaspoon salt
1/2 cup butter, softened
1/4 cup shortening
1 1/2 cups buttermilk
3 eggs
1 cup golden raisins, chopped
1/2 cup chopped walnuts
1 tablespoon orange zest
1 1/2 teaspoons vanilla extract

1 recipe Williamsburg Butter Frosting

Directions

Preheat oven to 350 degrees F (175 degrees C). Grease and flour a 9x13 inch pan, two 9 inch round cake pans, or three 8 inch round cake pans.

In a large bowl, combine cake flour, sugar, baking soda and salt. Mix in butter, shortening, buttermilk, eggs, raisins, nuts, orange zest and vanilla. Beat with an electric mixer for 3 minutes on high speed. Pour batter into prepared pan.

Bake in preheated oven until a toothpick inserted in center of cake comes out clean. Bake 9x13 inch pan 45 to 50 minutes, or layers 30 to 35 minutes. Allow to cool, and frost with Williamsburg Butter Frosting.

Peanut Butter Cake I

Ingredients

1/2 cup peanut butter
1/2 cup butter
1 cup packed brown sugar
1/2 cup white sugar
2 eggs
3/4 teaspoon vanilla extract
2 1/2 cups sifted all-purpose flour
3 teaspoons baking powder
1/2 teaspoon salt
1 cup milk
1/8 cup butter
3 cups confectioners' sugar
4 1/2 tablespoons evaporated milk
1 1/2 teaspoons vanilla extract

Directions

Preheat oven to 350 degrees F (175 degrees C). Grease and flour a 9x13 inch cake pan.

Cream together 1/2 cup butter and 1/2 cup peanut butter. Stir in white and brown sugars and beat well, then add the beaten eggs and 3/4 teaspoon of vanilla. Sift together flour, baking powder and salt. Add the flour mixture into the batter alternately with the milk.

Pour batter into the prepared pan and bake for 35 minutes. Frost when cool.

To Make Frosting: Blend together 1/8 cup butter or margarine, 3 cups confectioners' sugar, 4 1/2 tablespoons evaporated milk and 1 1/2 teaspoons vanilla extract, stirring slowly until mixture holds its shape. Then beat until very smooth. If necessary, gradually add tiny amounts of evaporated milk to bring to spreading consistency.

Pineapple Cake I

Ingredients

1 (18.25 ounce) package reduced fat yellow cake mix
1 (20 ounce) can crushed pineapple with juice
3 eggs

Directions

Preheat oven to 350 degrees F (175 degrees C). Spray a 9 x 13 inch pan with non-stick cooking spray.

Combine cake mix, pineapple (with juice), and eggs until well-mixed.

Pour into pan, and bake 30-35 minutes.

Lemon Sponge Cake II

Ingredients

7 egg whites
1/4 cup brown sugar
1/4 cup fructose (fruit sugar)
1/2 teaspoon salt

4 egg yolks
1/4 cup brown sugar
1/4 cup fructose (fruit sugar)
3/4 cup all-purpose flour
1/4 cup fresh lemon juice

Directions

Preheat oven to 350 degrees F (175 degrees C).Grease and flour a 10 inch tube pan.

In a large mixing bowl, combine the egg whites and salt. Whip with an electric mixer until soft peaks form. Continue mixing while gradually adding the 1/4 cup of brown sugar and fructose. Whip to stiff peaks, but not blocky.

In a medium bowl, combine the egg yolks, brown sugar and fructose. whip with an electric mixer until stiff and pale. Gradually mix in the lemon juice. Remove from mixer and fold sifter flour in by hand with a rubber spatula. Fold 1/3 of the egg whites into the yolk mixture until well blended, then fold the yolk mixture into the remaining egg whites. Pour batter evenly into the prepared pan.

Bake for 30 to 45 minutes in the preheated oven, until a toothpick inserted comes out clean. Allow the cake to cool for 10 minutes in the pan before inverting onto a wire rack to cool completely.

Carrot Cake I

Ingredients

3 cups grated carrots
4 eggs
1 1/4 cups vegetable oil
2 cups white sugar
2 cups sifted all-purpose flour
2 teaspoons baking powder
2 teaspoons baking soda
1 teaspoon ground cinnamon
1 teaspoon salt
1/2 teaspoon ground nutmeg
1 cup golden raisins
1 1/4 cups confectioners' sugar
1 (3 ounce) package cream cheese
1 tablespoon light corn syrup
1/2 teaspoon vanilla extract

Directions

Beat together the eggs, oil, and white sugar. Blend mixture for thirty seconds.

Sift together flour, baking powder, baking soda, salt and spices. Add the carrots and raisins. Pour egg mixture into dry ingredients, and mix well.

Pour batter into well greased 10 inch tube or bundt pan. Bake at 350 degrees F (175 degrees C) oven for 60 to 70 minutes. Cool cake on wire rack, and then refrigerate until completely cooled.

To make Cream Cheese Glaze: Blend together confectioners' sugar, cream cheese, corn syrup, and vanilla. Spread over cooled cake.

Diane's German Chocolate Cake

Ingredients

1 (18.25 ounce) package butter cake mix
1 (3.5 ounce) package instant vanilla pudding mix
1/3 cup unsweetened cocoa powder
1 cup buttermilk
1/3 cup vegetable oil
3 eggs
1 (12 fluid ounce) can evaporated milk
1 cup white sugar
1 cup chopped pecans
1 teaspoon vanilla extract
3 egg yolks
1/2 cup butter
1 cup flaked coconut

Directions

Preheat oven to 350 degrees F (175 degrees C). Grease and flour three 8 inch round cake pans.

Combine the cake mix, instant vanilla pudding, cocoa, buttermilk, vegetable oil and the 3 whole eggs. Mix until blended and pour the batter into the prepared pans.

Bake at 350 degrees F (175 degrees C) for 20 to 25 minutes or until the cakes test done. Set cakes aside to cool.

In a medium sized sauce pan mix the evaporated milk, white sugar, 3 egg yolks and the butter. Cook over medium heat until the mixture is thick. Remove from heat and beat until partially cooled. Beat in the vanilla. Stir in the flaked coconut and the chopped pecans. Use to fill and frost cake.

Dried Cherry Cake

Ingredients

1/2 cup chopped dried cherries
1/2 cup hot water
1/2 teaspoon almond extract
1 1/2 cups all-purpose flour
2 teaspoons baking powder
1/4 teaspoon salt
1 cup white sugar
1 (8 ounce) container vanilla yogurt
1/2 cup vegetable oil
1 egg
1 egg white
1/4 cup chopped pecans
1 tablespoon white sugar

Directions

Combine cherries, hot water, and almond extract: let stand 20 minutes. Drain cherries, and pat dry between layers of paper towels. Set aside.

In a large bowl, combine flour, salt, baking powder, and 1 cup white sugar. Add yogurt, eggs, and oil. Stir well. Fold in cherries. Pour batter into a greased and floured 9 inch round cake pan.

Stir pecans and 1 tablespoon white sugar together. Sprinkle on top of batter in pan.

Bake at 350 degrees F (175 degrees C) for 35 minutes, or until wooden pick comes out clean. Cool in pan on wire rack 10 minutes. Serve warm, or at room temperature.

Peach Pound Cake

Ingredients

1 cup butter (no substitutes), softened
2 cups sugar
6 eggs
1 teaspoon almond extract
1 teaspoon vanilla extract
3 cups all-purpose flour 1/4 teaspoon baking soda 1/4 teaspoon salt
1/2 cup sour cream
2 cups diced fresh or frozen peaches
confectioners' sugar

Directions

In a large mixing bowl, cream butter and sugar until light and fluffy. Add eggs, one at a time, beating well after each addition. Beat in extracts. combine the flour, baking soda and salt; add to the batter alternately with sour cream. Fold in the peaches.

Pour into a greased and floured 10-in. fluted tube pan. Bake at 350 degrees F for 60-70 minutes or until a toothpick inserted near the center comes out clean. cool for 15 minutes before removing from pan to a wire rack to cool completely. Dust with confectioners' sugar if desired.

German Sweet Chocolate Cake II

Ingredients

4 (1 ounce) squares German sweet chocolate, chopped
2/3 cup butter
1 1/2 cups white sugar
2 eggs
1 teaspoon vanilla extract
1 cup buttermilk
2 1/2 cups sifted cake flour
1/2 teaspoon baking powder
1 teaspoon baking soda
1/2 teaspoon salt

1 cup evaporated milk
1 cup white sugar
3 egg yolks, lightly beaten
1/2 cup butter
1 teaspoon vanilla extract
1 1/3 cups flaked coconut
1 cup chopped pecans

Directions

Preheat oven to 350 degrees F (175 degrees C). Grease and flour 3 (8 inch) round pans. Sift together the flour, baking powder, baking soda and salt. Set aside. In the top of a double boiler, heat chocolate, stirring occasionally, until chocolate is melted and smooth. Remove from heat and allow to cool to lukewarm.

In a large bowl, cream together the butter and 1 1/2 cups sugar until light and fluffy. Beat in the eggs one at a time, then stir in melted chocolate and 1 teaspoon vanilla. Beat in the flour mixture alternately with the buttermilk, mixing just until incorporated. Pour batter into prepared pans.

Bake in the preheated oven for 30 to 35 minutes, or until a toothpick inserted into the center of the cake comes out clean. Let cool in pans for 10 minutes, then turn out onto a wire rack and cool completely. When cool, frost between layers and on top of cake.

To make the Frosting: In a large saucepan, combine evaporated milk, 1 cup sugar, egg yolks, 1/2 cup butter and 1 teaspoon vanilla. Cook and stir on medium heat for about 12 minutes, or until thick and golden brown. Remove from heat. Stir in coconut and pecans. Cool to room temperature, and spreading consistency.

Piggy Pudding Dessert Cake

Ingredients

1/2 cup butter
1 1/2 cups all-purpose flour
1 cup chopped walnuts
1 (16 ounce) package frozen whipped topping, thawed
1 (8 ounce) package cream cheese
1 cup confectioners' sugar
1 (3.9 ounce) package instant chocolate pudding mix
3 cups milk
1/2 cup chopped walnuts

Directions

Preheat oven to 375 degrees F (190 degrees C).

In a medium bowl, combine butter or margarine, flour and chopped walnuts. Mix, then pat into bottom of 9x13 " pan.

Bake at 375 degrees F (190 degrees C) for 20 minutes. Allow to cool.

Beat softened cream cheese with confectioners sugar until smooth. Fold in 1/2 of the whipped topping. Spread over cooled crust.

In a medium bowl, combine chocolate pudding mix with 3 cups milk. Mix well and spread over cream cheese mixture.

Spread remaining 1/2 container of whipped topping over pudding. Sprinkle with 1/2 cup chopped nuts.

General Robert E. Lee Cake II

Ingredients

2 cups all-purpose flour
1/2 teaspoon cream of tartar
1 1/2 teaspoons baking powder
8 egg yolks
2 cups white sugar
8 egg whites
2 teaspoons grated lemon zest
2 tablespoons lemon juice
1/8 teaspoon salt

4 egg yolks
1 1/3 cups white sugar
2 1/2 teaspoons grated lemon zest
1/3 cup lemon juice
1/4 cup butter

1/3 cup butter, softened
4 cups confectioners' sugar
3 tablespoons grated orange zest
2 1/2 tablespoons orange juice
1 1/2 teaspoons grated lemon zest
1 1/2 tablespoons lemon juice
1/2 cup flaked coconut

Directions

Preheat oven to 325 degrees F (165 degrees C). Grease and flour two 9 inch pans. Sift together the flour, baking powder, and cream of tartar. Set aside.

In a medium bowl, beat together the 8 egg yolks and 2 cups sugar until thick and pale. Stir in the 2 teaspoons lemon zest and 2 tablespoons lemon juice. In a large glass or metal mixing bowl, beat egg whites and salt until soft peaks form. Fold whites into the egg yolk mixture alternately with the flour mixture. Spread evenly into the prepared pans.

Bake for 25 to 30 minutes in the preheated oven, or until a toothpick inserted into the cake comes out clean. Let layers cool in the pan for 15 minutes before inverting onto wire racks to cool completely. Using a long serrated knife, slice the layers in half horizontally.

To make the filling: In the top of a double boiler, combine the 1 1/3 cup sugar, 4 egg yolks, 2 1/2 teaspoon lemon zest and 1/3 cup lemon juice. Cook over high heat, stirring constantly, until the sugar is dissolved and mixture thickens. Remove from heat, and stir in the butter. Cool to room temperature before filling cake.

To make the frosting: In a medium bowl, cream the 1/3 cup butter until light and fluffy. Gradually add the confectioners sugar and mix in the orange zest, orange juice, lemon zest and lemon juice.
Finally, stir in coconut. Frost the outside of the filled cake.

White Chocolate Fudge Cake

Ingredients

1 (18.25 ounce) package white cake mix
1 1/4 cups water
3 egg whites
1/3 cup vegetable oil
1 teaspoon vanilla extract
3 (1 ounce) squares white chocolate, melted
FILLING:
3/4 cup semisweet chocolate chips
2 tablespoons butter (no substitutes)
FROSTING:
1 (16 ounce) can vanilla frosting
3 (1 ounce) squares white chocolate, melted
1 teaspoon vanilla extract
1 (8 ounce) carton frozen whipped topping, thawed

Directions

In a mixing bowl, combine the dry cake mix, water, egg whites, oil and vanilla. Beat on low for 2 minutes. Stir in white chocolate. Pour into a greased 13-in. x 9-in. x 2-in. baking pan. Bake at 350 degrees F for 25-30 minutes or until a toothpick inserted near the center comes out clean. Cool for 5 minutes.

Meanwhile, in a microwave or heavy saucepan over low heat, melt chocolate chips and butter; stir until smooth. Carefully spread over warm cake. Cool completely.

In a mixing bowl, beat frosting; stir in white chocolate and vanilla. Fold in whipped topping; frost cake. Store in the refrigerator.

Depression Cake III

Ingredients

2 cups strong brewed coffee
1 1/2 cups white sugar
1/2 cup butter
1 cup raisins
1 teaspoon ground allspice
1 teaspoon ground cinnamon
3 cups all-purpose flour
2 teaspoons baking soda
1 teaspoon baking powder

Directions

Preheat oven to 350 degrees F (175 degrees C). Grease and flour a 9x13 inch pan. Sift together the flour, baking soda and baking powder. Set aside.

In a large saucepan combine the coffee, sugar, butter, raisins, allspice and cinnamon. Bring to a boil, remove from heat and set aside to cool to room temperature.

Stir in flour mixture until well combined. Pour into a 9x13 inch pan. Bake in preheated oven for 45 to 50 minutes, or until a toothpick inserted into the center of cake comes out clean.

Whiskey Cake II

Ingredients

1 (18.25 ounce) package yellow cake mix
1 (3.4 ounce) package instant vanilla pudding mix
5 eggs
1/2 cup milk
1/2 cup whiskey
3/4 cup butter, cut into pieces
1 (11 ounce) package butterscotch chips
1 cup chopped walnuts

Directions

Preheat oven to 350 degrees F (175 degrees C). Grease and flour a 9x13 inch pan.

In a large bowl, stir together cake mix and pudding mix. Make a well in the center and pour in eggs, milk, whiskey and butter. Beat on low speed until blended. Scrape bowl, and beat 4 minutes on medium speed. Reserve a 1/4 cup each of the butterscotch chips and walnuts for the top of the cake. Stir in the remaining butterscotch chips and walnuts to the batter. Pour batter into prepared pan and sprinkle with reserved chips and nuts.

Pour batter into prepared pan. Bake in the preheated oven for 50 to 60 minutes, or until a toothpick inserted into the center of the cake comes out clean. Allow to cool.

Mafioso Chocolate Cake

Ingredients

1/2 cup Dutch process cocoa powder
3/4 cup boiling water
1 cup sour cream
1/2 teaspoon baking soda
2 cups sifted cake flour
1/2 cup butter
2 cups white sugar
3 egg whites
1 1/2 teaspoons vanilla extract
6 tablespoons butter, softened
3/4 cup Dutch process cocoa powder
2 2/3 cups confectioners' sugar
1/2 cup milk
1 teaspoon vanilla extract

Directions

In a small bowl, mix together 1/2 cup cocoa and 3/4 cup boiling water; set aside.

In another small bowl, dissolve baking soda in the sour cream by stirring them together.

In a large bowl, cream the 1/2 cup butter and 2 cups sugar. To the butter and sugar mixture, alternately add the sifted flour and the cocoa mixture with the sour cream mixture. Beat until fluffy. Beat the egg whites until stiff and fold in the egg whites and 1 1/2 teaspoons of vanilla.

Grease a 9x13 inch pan and pour the batter into it. Bake at 300 degrees F (150 degrees C) for 50 minutes. Frost with La Famiglia Chocolate Frosting (below).

To Make La Famiglia Chocolate Frosting: Cream 6 tablespoons butter or margarine in a small bowl.   Add 3/4 cup cocoa and confectioner's sugar alternately with milk; beat until spreading consistency. More or less milk can be used depending on the texture you want. Blend in the vanilla. This yields about 2 cups of frosting.

Rhubarb Pineapple Upside-Down Cake

Ingredients

1 (20 ounce) can crushed pineapple, drained with juice reserved
3 cups chopped rhubarb
1/2 cup white sugar
1/2 cup packed brown sugar
1 (3 ounce) package strawberry flavored gelatin
2 cups miniature marshmallows
1 (18.25 ounce) package white cake mix

Directions

Preheat the oven to 350 degrees F (175 degrees C). Grease a 9x13 inch baking dish.

In a medium bowl, mix together the pineapple, rhubarb, white sugar, brown sugar, gelatin, and marshmallows. Pour evenly in the bottom of the prepared pan. In the same bowl, prepare the cake mix according to package directions, substituting the reserved pineapple juice for the as much water in the recipe as you can. pour over the fruit, and spread evenly.

Bake for 1 hour in the preheated oven, or until a toothpick inserted into the center of the cake comes out clean. Invert the cake onto a serving platter while still warm, or cut into pieces, and turn upside-down when serving.

Dark Chocolate Cream Cheese Cake

Ingredients

3 cups all-purpose flour
2 cups white sugar
1/2 cup unsweetened cocoa powder
2 teaspoons baking soda
1/2 teaspoon salt
2 cups hot water
1 tablespoon instant coffee powder
2/3 cup vegetable oil
2 tablespoons white vinegar
2 teaspoons vanilla extract
2 eggs
1/4 cup white sugar

1 (8 ounce) package cream cheese
1/4 cup white sugar
1/2 teaspoon vanilla extract
1 egg
1 cup semisweet chocolate chips
1 cup finely chopped walnuts

Directions

Preheat oven to 350 degrees F (175 degrees C).Grease and flour a 9x13 inch pan.

In a large bowl, stir together the flour, sugar, cocoa, baking soda and salt. Combine the hot water and instant coffee, then add to the dry ingredients along with the oil, vinegar, vanilla and eggs. Mix until smooth and well blended. Spread batter evenly into the prepared pan. Sprinkle with the 1/4 cup of sugar.

Bake for 45 to 60 minutes in the preheated oven, until a toothpick inserted comes out clean.

Make the topping while the cake is cooling. In a medium-size mixing bowl, beat together the cream cheese, sugar, vanilla and egg until smooth. Stir in the chocolate chips and walnuts. Spread over cooled cake.

Spicy Apple Cake

Ingredients

1/2 cup shortening
1 cup brown sugar
1/4 cup white sugar
2 eggs
1 teaspoon vanilla extract
1 1/2 cups all-purpose flour
1 teaspoon baking powder
1/2 teaspoon baking soda
1/2 teaspoon salt
1 teaspoon ground cinnamon
1/2 teaspoon ground nutmeg
1/2 cup milk
2 cups apple - peeled, cored, and chopped
1/4 cup shortening
2 cups sifted confectioners' sugar
1/4 teaspoon ground cinnamon
1 pinch ground nutmeg
1/4 cup evaporated milk

Directions

Preheat oven to 350 degrees F (175 degrees C). Grease and flour a 9 inch square pan. Sift together the flour, baking powder, baking soda, salt, cinnamon and nutmeg. Set aside.

In a large bowl, cream together the shortening, brown sugar and white sugar until light and fluffy. Beat in the eggs one at a time, then stir in the vanilla. Beat in the flour mixture alternately with the milk, mixing just until incorporated. Stir in the chopped apples.

Spread batter evenly in prepared pan. Bake in the preheated oven for 35 to 40 minutes, or until a toothpick inserted into the center of the cake comes out clean. Allow to cool.

To make the frosting: In a medium bowl, combine 1/4 cup shortening, confectioners' sugar, cinnamon and nutmeg. Beat until light and creamy. Beat in the milk, one tablespoon at a time, until desired spreading consistency is achieved. Spread over top of cooled cake.

Sour Cream Pound Cake

Ingredients

1 1/2 cups all-purpose flour
1 1/2 cups white sugar
1/2 cup butter
1/2 cup sour cream
3 eggs
1 pinch baking soda

Directions

Preheat oven to 375 degrees F (190 degrees C). Grease and flour a 8x4 inch loaf pan.

In a large bowl, cream butter and sugar until light and fluffy. Add sour cream and eggs.

Add flour and pinch of soda, mix well. Pour into a 8x4 inch loaf pan.

Bake at 375 degrees F (190 degrees C) for 1 hour, or until a toothpick inserted into center of cake comes out clean.

Sock it to Me Cake II

Ingredients

1 (18.25 ounce) package butter cake mix
4 eggs
2 cups sour cream
1 teaspoon vanilla extract
1 cup white sugar
2/3 cup vegetable oil
1 cup chopped pecans
1/2 cup butter
1 cup white sugar
1/2 cup buttermilk
1 teaspoon baking soda
1 teaspoon ground cinnamon
3/4 cup packed brown sugar

Directions

Mix together the cake mix and eggs. Fold in the sour cream. Mix in the vanilla, 1 cup sugar, oil and pecans.

Pour half of batter into a 9 x 13 inch pan. Combine the ground cinammon and brown sugar. Sprinkle over the batter. Pour the other half of the batter over top.

Bake at 350 degrees F (175 degrees C) for 50 minutes.

To make Icing: Bring to a boil 1/2 cup butter or margarine, 1 cup sugar, buttermilk and baking soda. Prick cake all over with fork and pour hot icing on cake.

Spiced Farmhouse Fairy Cakes

Ingredients

3/4 cup superfine sugar
1/2 cup margarine
2 eggs
1 teaspoon cinnamon
1 pinch ginger
1 1/2 cups self-rising flour
1/4 cup confectioners' sugar
1 pinch cardamom (optional)

Directions

Preheat the oven to 350 degrees F (175 degrees C). Lay out about 18 cupcake (muffin) papers on a baking sheet or place them in a muffin pan.

In a medium bowl, cream together the sugar and margarine until light and fluffy. Beat in the eggs one at a time using an electric mixer, or the whole thing may be mixed in a blender. Add cinnamon and ginger to the batter and mix well. Stir in the flour until well blended. Spoon a generous tablespoon of the batter into each paper, and level it out.

Bake for 15 to 20 minutes in the preheated oven, until the tops spring back when lightly pressed. Dust with confectioners' sugar and cardamom when cooled.

Zucchini Cake III

Ingredients

4 eggs
2 cups white sugar
1 cup vegetable oil
2 cups all-purpose flour
2 teaspoons ground cinnamon
1 teaspoon salt
2 teaspoons baking powder
1 teaspoon baking soda
1 (8 ounce) can crushed pineapple, drained
1 cup chopped walnuts
2 cups grated zucchini
2 teaspoons vanilla extract
1 cup confectioners' sugar
2 tablespoons milk

Directions

Preheat oven to 350 degrees F (175 degrees C). Grease and flour a tube pan.

Sift together flour, cinnamon, salt, baking powder, and baking soda on to a piece of waxed paper.

In a large bowl, beat eggs and sugar until light colored. Mix in oil. Add sifted ingredients to egg mixture, and beat for 2 minutes. Stir in pineapple, chopped nuts, vanilla, and zucchini. Mix thoroughly. Pour batter into prepared pan.

Bake for 80 minutes, or until tester inserted in the center of the cake comes out clean. Cool for 30 minutes.

To Make Glaze: In a small bowl, combine the confectioners' sugar and the milk.   When cake has cooled, pour glaze over cake.

Snickerdoodle Cake II

Ingredients

1/4 cup white sugar
1/2 teaspoon ground cinnamon
1 tablespoon butter
1 3/4 cups all-purpose flour
2 1/2 teaspoons baking powder
1/2 cup white sugar
1/4 cup shortening
1 egg
3/4 cup milk

Directions

Preheat oven to 350 degrees F (175 degrees C). Grease and flour an 8 inch square pan. Make topping by mixing 1/4 cup sugar and 1/2 teaspoon cinnamon with 1 tablespoon butter. Set aside.

In a large bowl mix flour, baking powder and 1/2 cup sugar. Cut in shortening to a fine grain. In a separate small bowl beat egg, then pour in milk and mix together. Beat into dry mixture with minimum of strokes.

Spread batter into prepared pan and sprinkle with topping. Bake in the preheated oven for 20 to 25 minutes, or until a toothpick inserted into the center of the cake comes out clean. Serve warm.

Easter Lamb Cake

Ingredients

1 (18.25 ounce) package white cake mix
1 (16 ounce) can white frosting
3 cups flaked coconut
2 black jellybeans
1 black shoestring licorice
2 drops green food coloring

Directions

Prepare cake mix according to package directions and bake in two halves of a stand-up lamb cake pan. Cool completely.

Stick the two halves of the lamb together using white frosting. Sit the lamb up and frost the entire lamb. Coat the entire lamb with coconut. Decorate with jelly beans for eyes, and licorice for whiskers. Tint any remaining coconut with green food color and use as grass.

Herman Coffee Cake

Ingredients

2 cups Herman Sourdough Starter
2/3 cup vegetable oil
2 eggs
2 cups all-purpose flour
1 1/2 teaspoons ground cinnamon
1/2 teaspoon baking soda
2 teaspoons baking powder
1/2 teaspoon salt
1 cup white sugar
1 cup chopped pecans
1 cup raisins
1 cup packed brown sugar
3 tablespoons all-purpose flour
1 teaspoon ground cinnamon
1/4 cup margarine, softened
1/2 cup margarine
1/4 cup milk
1 cup packed brown sugar

Directions

Bring Herman Starter to room temperature.

Preheat oven to 350 degrees F (175 degrees C). Grease and lightly flour one 9x13 inch baking pan.

Stir together Herman Starter, oil and beaten eggs.

Stir together the flour, cinnamon, baking soda, baking powder, salt and white sugar. Stir in nuts and raisins. Add the flour mixture to the egg mixture and stir well. Pour into the prepared pan and sprinkle with the topping.

To Make Topping: Combine the 1 cup brown sugar, 3 tablespoons flour, 1 teaspoon cinnamon. Cut in 1/4 cup softened butter, until the mixture resembles very coarse crumbs.

Bake in a preheated 350 degrees F (175 degrees C) for 30 to 40 minutes. While still hot pour glaze over the top and serve.

To Make Glaze: In a small saucepan, melt 1/2 cup butter or margarine. Stir in the milk and 1 cup brown sugar. Bring to a boil and let boil for 3 minutes. Immediately pour over hot cake.

Million Dollar Cake

Ingredients

1 (18.25 ounce) package yellow cake mix
8 ounces cream cheese
1 1/2 cups confectioners' sugar
1 (20 ounce) can crushed pineapple with juice
2 (8 ounce) cans mandarin oranges, drained
1 (3.5 ounce) package instant vanilla pudding mix
1 (8 ounce) container frozen whipped topping, thawed

Directions

Mix and bake cake mix as per package instruction for two 8 or 9 inch round layers. Let layers cool, and then split each layer in half so as to have 4 layers.

In a large bowl, whip cream cheese until soft, and then gradually mix in confectioners' sugar. Stir in the pineapple with juice and the drained mandarin oranges, reserving about 5 mandarin orange slices to decorate the top of cake. Mix in the dry pudding mix. Fold in the whipped topping.

Place one cake layer on a cake plate cut side up; spread with frosting. Place another layer cut side down on the first one, and top with more frosting. Repeat until all layers are used, spreading last bit of frosting on top and sides of cake. Decorate with reserved mandarin orange slices. Refrigerate overnight before serving.

Chocolate Chip Amaretto Pound Cake

Ingredients

3 eggs
1 (18.25 ounce) package devil's food cake mix
1/3 cup vegetable oil
1 cup water
2 tablespoons almond extract
1 cup semisweet chocolate chips
1/4 cup confectioners' sugar for dusting

Directions

Preheat the oven to 350 degrees F (175 degrees C). Grease the bundt pan.

Mix eggs, cake mix, oil, water and almond extract with electric beater. Stir in chocolate chips.

Pour into prepared pan. Bake approximately 1 hour or until cake tests done. Cool, then dust with confectioners' sugar.

Chocolate Mousse Cake V

Ingredients

12 1/2 ounces bittersweet chocolate, chopped
1/8 cup unsalted butter
12 egg yolks
1/4 cup white sugar
12 egg whites
1/8 cup white sugar
1 1/4 cups heavy cream
1 tablespoon unsweetened cocoa powder, for dusting

Directions

Preheat oven to 300 degrees F (150 degrees C). Butter a 9 inch springform pan, and line bottom with parchment paper.

In the top of a double boiler, heat chocolate and unsalted butter, stirring occasionally, until chocolate is melted and smooth. Remove from heat and allow to cool to lukewarm.

In a large bowl, beat egg yolks and 1/4 cup sugar until thick and lemon-colored. Fold into chocolate mixture; set aside. In a large glass or metal mixing bowl, beat egg whites until foamy. Gradually add 1/8 cup sugar, continuing to beat until stiff peaks form. Fold 1/3 of the whites into the chocolate mixture, then quickly fold in remaining whites until no streaks remain. Pour 2/3 of mixture into prepared pan.

Bake in the preheated oven for 40 minutes, or until filling is just firm in the center. Allow to cool, then remove from pan and refrigerate 1 hour.

In a medium bowl, whip cream to soft peaks and fold into remaining chocolate mixture. Cover and refrigerate.

Spread remaining mousse over cooled cake and dust with cocoa.

Red Velvet Cake IV

Ingredients

1 cup butter, softened
3 cups white sugar
6 eggs
1 ounce red food coloring
3 tablespoons unsweetened cocoa powder
3 cups all-purpose flour
1 cup buttermilk
1 teaspoon vanilla extract
1/2 teaspoon salt
1 teaspoon baking soda
1 tablespoon white vinegar

2 (8 ounce) packages cream cheese
12 ounces white chocolate
1 cup butter, softened

Directions

Preheat oven to 325 degrees F (165 degrees C). Grease and flour three 8 inch pans.

In a large bowl, cream 1 cup butter with sugar. Add eggs one at a time, beating well after each addition. Mix food coloring with cocoa and add to mixture.

Add flour alternately with buttermilk. Add vanilla and salt.

Mix baking soda with vinegar, and gently stir into mixture. Be careful not to over mix.

Divide batter into three prepared 8 inch round pans. Bake at 325 degrees F (165 degrees C) for 25 minutes. Allow to cool.

To make the White Chocolate Cream Cheese Icing: Melt the white chocolate and allow to cool to lukewarm. In a large bowl, beat the cream cheese until light and fluffy. Gradually beat in melted white chocolate and softened butter. Beat until it is the consistency of whipped cream, then use to fill and frost the cake.

Dee's Hot Milk Sponge Cake

Ingredients

3/4 cup milk
2 tablespoons butter
3 eggs
1 1/2 cups white sugar
1 1/2 cups all-purpose flour
1 1/2 teaspoons baking powder
1 teaspoon vanilla extract

Directions

Preheat oven to 350 degrees F (175 degrees C). Grease one large loaf pan or one 10 inch tube pan.

In a saucepan over medium-low heat the milk and the butter. Do not boil.

In a large bowl beat the eggs until light colored. Gradually add the sugar to the eggs then stir in the flour and baking powder. Stir in the hot milk and butter. Beat only until combined. Stir in the vanilla.
Pour the batter into the prepared pan.

Bake at 350 degrees F (175 degrees C) for 45 to 50 minutes. Let cake cool in pan for 10 minutes. Remove cake from the pan and cool on a wire rack.

Margarita Cake

Ingredients

1 (18.25 ounce) package orange cake mix
1 (3.4 ounce) package instant vanilla pudding mix
4 eggs
1/2 cup vegetable oil
2/3 cup water
1/4 cup lemon juice
1/4 cup tequila
2 tablespoons triple sec liqueur

1 cup confectioners' sugar
1 tablespoon tequila
2 tablespoons triple sec liqueur
2 tablespoons lime juice

Directions

Preheat oven to 350 degrees F (175 degrees C). Grease and flour a 10 inch Bundt pan.

In a large bowl combine cake mix, pudding mix, eggs, oil, water, lemon juice 1/4 cup tequila and 2 tablespoons triple sec. Beat for 2 minutes.

Pour batter into prepared pan. Bake in the preheated oven for 45 to 50 minutes, or until a toothpick inserted into the center of the cake comes out clean. Cool in pan for 10 minutes; remove to rack and pour glaze over cake while still warm.

To make the glaze: In a small bowl, combine confectioners' sugar with 1 tablespoon tequila, 2 tablespoons triple sec and 2 tablespoons lime juice. Mix until smooth.

Elvis Presley Cake

Ingredients

1 (18.25 ounce) package white cake mix
1 (8 ounce) can crushed pineapple with juice
2 cups white sugar
1 (8 ounce) package cream cheese
1/2 cup butter, softened
4 cups confectioners' sugar
1 teaspoon vanilla extract
1 cup chopped pecans

Directions

Prepare cake according to instructions on package. Bake in a 9x13 inch pan. Allow to cool.

Combine pineapple and sugar in saucepan. Bring to a boil. Spoon over cooled cake.

In a large bowl, cream butter and cream cheese until smooth. Add powdered sugar and beat until smooth. Add vanilla. Add pecans and mix well.

Spread cream cheese frosting over cake.

Cherry Chocolate Marble Cake

Ingredients

1 cup butter or margarine, softened
2 cups sugar
3 eggs
6 tablespoons maraschino cherry juice
6 tablespoons water
1 teaspoon almond extract
3 3/4 cups all-purpose flour
2 1/4 teaspoons baking soda
3/4 teaspoon salt
1 1/2 cups sour cream
3/4 cup chopped maraschino cherries, drained
3/4 cup chopped walnuts, toasted
3 (1 ounce) squares unsweetened chocolate, melted
confectioners' sugar

Directions

In a mixing bowl, cream butter and sugar. Add the eggs, one at a time, beating well after each addition. Add the cherry juice, water and extract; mix well. Combine flour, baking soda and salt; add to creamed mixture alternately with sour cream. Mix just until combined.

Divide batter in half. to one portion, add cherries and walnuts; mix well. To the second portion, add chocolate; mix well. Spoon half of the cherry mixture into a greased and floured 10-in. fluted tube pan. Cover with half of the chocolate mixture. Repeat layers. Bake at 350 degrees F for 1 hour and 15 minutes or until a toothpick inserted near the center comes out clean. Cool for 15 minutes; remove from pan to a wire rack to cool completely. Dust with confectioners; sugar if desired.

Rhubarb Pudding Cake

Ingredients

3 cups diced fresh or frozen rhubarb
1 cup all-purpose flour
3/4 cup sugar
1/3 cup milk
3 tablespoons butter or margarine, melted
1 teaspoon baking powder
1/4 teaspoon salt
1/4 teaspoon vanilla extract
TOPPING:
1 cup sugar
1 tablespoon cornstarch
1 cup boiling water
1/2 teaspoon ground cinnamon

Directions

Place rhubarb in a greased 8-in. square baking pan. In a small bowl, mix flour, sugar, milk, butter, baking powder, salt and vanilla (mixture will be stiff). Spread over rhubarb. For topping, combine sugar and cornstarch. Sprinkle over dough. Pour water over all; do not stir. Sprinkle cinnamon on top. Bake at 350 degrees F for 55-65 minutes or until pudding tests done.

Butter Pecan Cake

Ingredients

3 tablespoons butter or margarine, melted
1 1/3 cups chopped pecans
2/3 cup butter or margarine, softened
1 1/3 cups sugar
2 eggs
2 cups all-purpose flour
1 1/2 teaspoons baking powder
1/4 teaspoon salt
2/3 cup milk
1 1/2 teaspoons vanilla extract
BUTTER PECAN FROSTING:
3 tablespoons butter or margarine, softened
3 cups confectioners' sugar
3 tablespoons milk
3/4 teaspoon vanilla extract

Directions

Pour melted butter into a baking pan. Stir in pecans. Toast at 350 degrees F for 10 minutes. Set aside to cool.

In a mixing bowl, cream butter and sugar until light and fluffy. Add eggs, one at a time, beating well after each addition. Combine flour, baking powder and salt; add to creamed mixture alternately with milk, beginning and ending with dry ingredients. Stir in vanilla and 1 cup toasted pecans. Pour batter into two greased and floured 8-in. round cake pans. Bake at 350 degrees F for 30-35 minutes or until the cakes test done. Cool in pans 5 minutes. Remove from pans and cool thoroughly on wire rack.

Meanwhile, for frosting, cream butter and sugar. Add milk and vanilla, beating until light and fluffy. Add additional milk if needed. Stir in remaining toasted pecans. Spread between the layers and over the top and sides of the cake.

Ingredients

2 cups packed brown sugar
2 cups hot water
2 tablespoons bacon grease
2 cups raisins
3 cups all-purpose flour
1 teaspoon salt
1 teaspoon baking soda
1 teaspoon ground cinnamon
1 teaspoon ground cloves

Directions

In a medium saucepan combine the brown sugar, hot water, bacon grease, and raisins, over medium heat. Bring to a boil for 5 minutes, then set aside to cool.

Preheat oven to 325 degrees F (165 degrees C). Grease and flour two 8x4 inch loaf pans.

In a large bowl, stir together the flour, salt, baking soda, cinnamon, and cloves. Add the ingredients from the saucepan and mix until well blended. Divide evenly between the two prepared pans.

Bake for 45 to 50 minutes in the preheated oven. Cool in pans for 10 minutes before removing to a wire rack to cool completely.

Chocolate Rum Cake

Ingredients

1 (18.25 ounce) package
chocolate cake mix
1 (3.9 ounce) package instant
chocolate pudding mix
4 eggs
1/2 cup water
1/2 cup vegetable oil
1/2 cup white rum
1/2 cup chopped nuts
1/2 cup butter
1 cup white sugar
1/4 cup white rum
1/4 cup water

Directions

Preheat oven to 325 degrees F (165 degrees C). Grease one 10 inch
bundt pan. Place chopped nuts in the bottom of the bundt pan.

With an electric mixer beat cake mix, pudding mix, eggs, oil, 1/2
cup of the water, and 1/2 cup of the rum on high speed for 2
minutes. Pour batter over into prepared pan over the top of the
chopped nuts.

Bake at 325 degrees F (165 degrees C) for 50 to 60 minutes. Pour
rum glaze over cake as soon as you remove it from the oven. Let
cake stand for 30 minutes then turn out onto a serving dish.

To Make Rum Glaze: In a saucepan combine the butter or
margarine, sugar, 1/4 cup of the rum, and 1/4 cup of the water.
Bring mixture to a boil and cook for 2 minutes. Pour immediately
over still warm cake.

Dairy Free Cinnamon Streusel Coffee Cake

Ingredients

1/3 cup dairy free pancake mix
(such as BisquickB®)
1/3 cup packed brown sugar
1/2 teaspoon ground cinnamon
3 tablespoons unsalted margarine

2 cups dairy free pancake mix
(such as BisquickB®)
2/3 cup soy milk
2 tablespoons white sugar
1 egg, lightly beaten

Directions

Preheat oven to 375 degrees F (190 degrees C). Grease an 8-inch square baking pan and set aside.

To make the streusel, combine 1/3 cup pancake mix, brown sugar, and cinnamon in a mixing bowl. Cut it the margarine until mixture is crumbly. (This can also be done in the food processor: pulse mixture 2 to 3 times to combine.)

Stir together the 2 cups of pancake mix, soy milk, sugar, and egg just until combined. Spread into prepared pan. Sprinkle with cinnamon streusel.

Bake in preheated oven for 20 to 25 minutes, or until a toothpick inserted into the center of the cake comes out clean. Cool before serving.